Relationship

MAITREYA 5

Shambhala
Berkeley & London
1974

MAITREYA is published by
SHAMBHALA PUBLICATIONS, INC.
2045 Francisco Street
Berkeley, California 94709

Editor: Hazel Silber Bercholz
Cover Calligraphy: Robert Steiner
Typography: Mercury Typography, Inc. &
 Arif Press
Cover Design: Based on a painting by
 Jordan Stenberg

The whole contents of MAITREYA are
Copyrighted© 1974 Shambhala Publications,
Inc.
All Rights Reserved
ISBN 0-87773-060-1
LCC 74-75101

Distributed in the United States by
RANDOM HOUSE
Distributed in the Commonwealth and Europe
by ROUTLEDGE & KEGAN PAUL, LTD.
London & Henley-on-Thames

Printed in the United States of America

Acknowledgments:
Photograph of Maitreya statue by Dominique Darbois from *The Cave Temples of Maichishan.* (Berkeley: University of California Press.)
"No Ox" page 17 by Arthur Okamura from *Oxherding.* (San Francisco: Cranium Press.)
Illustrations pages 18 & 35 by Armando Busick
Mandalas pages 49 & 90 by Jordan Stenberg
Etching page 50 by Josie Grant
"The Seven Caves from the Toltec legend of the original home of the race" page 70 from *Sensitive Chaos.* (London: Rudolf Steiner Press.)
Illustrations pages 71 & 73 from *On Growth and Form.* (Cambridge: The University Press.)
All illustrations in "Patterns of Greater Reality" by the author
Illustrations pages 93, 94, 98 by the author
"When Speaking on Different Subjects" from *Views from the Real World, Early Talks of Gurdjieff As Recollected by his Pupils.* Copyright© 1973 by Triangle Editions, Inc. Reprinted by permission of the publishers, E. P. Dutton & Co., Inc. (New York); Routledge & Kegan Paul, Ltd. (London)

Contents

- 9   Vincent Stuart/*Are There Any Questions?*
- 15   Chögyam Trungpa/*Relationship*
- 19   Charles Poncé/*An Alchemical Allegory: Notes Towards an Understanding of Genesis*
- 31   Ruth Hoebel/*Relationship: The Ship of Fools*
- 36   Diane di Prima/*Love Song of the Loba & The Loba Continues to Sing*
- 39   Herbert V. Guenther/*The Teacher and the Student*
- 51   René Daumal/*Memorables*
- 53   Graham Parkes/*Being Related*
- 56   Sully Prudhomme/*L'Habitude*
- 57   George I. Gurdjieff/*When Speaking on Different Subjects*
- 71   Gary Snyder/*Toward Climax*
- 75   George Doczi/*Patterns of Greater Reality*
- 91   Robert Hargrove/*Communion to Community*
- 93   Rowena Pattee/*Our Living Earth: A Vision of our Relationship with Nature*

Are There Any Questions?

Vincent Stuart

Is it, at the present time, an act of compassion or of irresponsibility to make known publicly the esoteric teachings that previously used to be given privately by a teacher to a pupil, according to the teacher's insight into the pupil's capacity to receive?

Why was it once considered necessary for esoteric teachings to be kept secret, and why are so many traditionally esoteric teachings now made known exoterically, throughout the world? Apart from such reasons as protection from possible persecution by the State Police and as a heresy by exoteric Churches, were there and are there valid reasons, concerned with the nature and purpose of the teaching itself and the intimate relationship between a teacher and a pupil, why privacy should be maintained? If there were such reasons, are they still valid and are they being unobserved at the cost of abasing the value of the teachings and their potential power to indicate how mankind may be regenerated? Or is the world at such a critical moment that it is urgently necessary for all teachings to be proclaimed aloud?

Are these questions answerable by minds still under the power of the senses? By minds lacking objective insight? What kind of person can apply a teaching to his being so as to understand the knowledge and awaken to a new mind? Does he or she need some attribute that is part of birthright, or can a new mind be awakened by acquisition of the knowledge available at schools, universities and training colleges, by means of a vast accumulation of knowledge derived from man's historical experience and discoveries on this planet? Does any amount of logical knowledge bring psycho-logical knowledge? Is not intellectual knowledge mistakenly assumed to be consciousness?

What is esoteric teaching about? What or who is its subject? How does it differ from ordinary knowledge?

Do not ideas conduct to, and among, mankind forces with the power to transform not only our values and habits, but our whole being, either through awakening our conscience and consciousness, or by deferring and debauching the latent evolution of our humanity? If the kind of ideas known as "esoteric teachings" have the virtue, commonly ascribed to them, to effect the transformation of man asleep into man awake is it necessarily implied that all mankind would awaken upon hearing or reading a teaching? That everyone can hear and see now?

Isn't it more likely to be true, from the evidence of historical records, that very few people in each generation have been able to understand a teaching sufficiently to undergo the re–birth, illumination, awakening, development of consciousness proferred to them? Is it just or unjust to conclude that it is wasteful, if not pointless, to spread abroad ideas that are received only by a few and which fertilize only a few? Doesn't the parable of the sower and the seed define in exact symbol three kinds of people who can, in different degree, hear a teaching, three levels of being, and three results from giving a teaching to these three kinds of people?[1] In its robustness is this parable not making it clear that there are only three kinds of people able to hear a teaching; that of these three only two will evolve in his inner being, and of the two only one kind of person can see things as they really are? While the rest of humanity, no matter for what reason, will, in that part of them from which growth is possible, be unaffected by a teaching? If so few people can, and wish, to receive a teaching would it not be right to conclude, therefore, that it is certainly wasteful and pointless to sow it widely and that the present practice of doing so is irresponsible?

By asking questions in terms of "either . . . or"—it being the habit of the logical, sense-based mind to assume that questions which are answerable reduce themselves to either one or the other of two ponderables—are not answers to psycho–logical questions always incorrectly answered by the logical mind? Why should this be so if the logical mind is the instrument to which mankind owes its material advantages? Are not its powers of reasoning and deduction enough for our evolution? But, then, doesn't esoteric teaching state, in one way or another, that an individual does not evolve through acquisition of knowledge about the physical world alone, because we are something else in addition to our bodies and their sensual faculties? That a third talent called, variously, essence, spirit, real self, and so on, must be at least partially active before esoteric teachings, that are not in terms of "either . . . or" but in terms of "yes *and* no," can be heard? In other words, that a person has to have an intuitive, spiritual, psycho–logical, cognitive mind, a chalice into which to receive a teaching? And to be able to recognize, sooner or later, that this receptive faculty is so seldom the right way up that his life for the most part is a complex but repetitive habit of reactions of the so-called logical mind, of the emotions and of the instincts, as they have been programmed since birth? If a person should feel that it matters to distinguish between sleep, unconsciousness, and being awake, consciousness, would there be any chance of doing so if he did not already have within him a seed, a grain of consciousness that can develop? Doesn't the parable of the sower and the seed affirm this to be so? If not to the logically-minded, to the people called materialists, then perhaps, or assuredly, to the cognitive person who has verified his own insight?

If we have recognized in ourselves states of sleep and states of being less asleep, and even states of momentary awakening, are we not verifying for ourselves that many different *levels* of being are present within us, and that the quality and character of our life accords with the level of being at which we are? Do we have an idea of on how few of the possible levels of being we live? If we were to realize this much would we not also acknowledge that our life at every one moment is a state of being that attracts and experiences both inner and outer events conforming to the level of being we are on? That is, levels have their concomitant states, so that to understand what transformation of being means it is necessary to realize that our life, while asleep, is mechanically dependent upon the level of being we are at? At which rung of Jacob's ladder are we?

So is not "being" as it were a scale of levels from coarse to fine, from "lead" to "gold," with all the qualities of every level within us, but unrealized until our consciousness has awakened to comprehend them all together in harmonious unity?

Perhaps we accept this intellectually and reject it emotionally because our concern for everything we feel to be ourselves insists on justifying its preservation? Yet can there be any real awakening and transformation of our consciousness as long as ego-centeredness is defended?

Can we know anybody without knowing ourselves? Can we know ourselves until our own invisibility becomes known to our consciousness? There is an apparent relationship of a person to something supposedly himself, to what a person imagines himself or herself to be, but isn't this a case of the blind leading the deaf, or the deaf leading the blind, rather than the realization of a person's whole consciousness and comprehension of every level of being within Being? Or as Shakespeare wrote: "To thine own self be true, and it must follow, as the night the day thou cans't not then be false to any man." Were we to begin to be true to ourselves would we not begin to have not only an understanding of our own multiplicity of being but also of the invisibility of other people to the extent, possibly, of realizing that "we do not like one another, we do not love one another; we are one another?"

Is there not much more in the aim of an esoteric teaching than the awakening of individuals? Isn't this but the first, or only one of, the aims? Isn't it concerned with the transformation of our relationships to one another, from these being a merely mechanical liking and disliking, to seeing ourself in the other and the other in ourself, in full acceptance? And if these two aims were realized would not a third be accomplished, namely a transformation in the level of being of all mankind, of Adam? Unless all three aims of esoteric teachings are valued will even one be active? Isn't seeking only one's own illumination nothing more than a symptom of self-love? Or is there a saving grace in this?

What do we make of our knowledge? Is there a factor, in any way governing the use of our knowledge, that we can recognize in ourselves and in others? Surely in every teaching there is much said about this, but do we take notice of it, do we see for ourselves that it is the average level of being which governs the use of our knowledge? What, in turn, influences being? Is it what is called conscience? If so, if conscience were all it is supposed to be as a power for well being, why are there so many quarrels, disputes, revenges, wars, so much hypocrisy, etc.; why are there so many different, conflicting "consciences?" Or is there a universal conscience? If there is, is it accessible to our sleeping consciousness? Perhaps a universal conscience is the attribute of a conscious person whose knowledge and being are fully developed, enabling him to do what he knows and who wills what he is? Who, being whole, radiates a force to all who, although yet houses divided against themselves, are ready to find within themselves their own "teacher"?

To begin with does not an external teacher and his teaching represent for us outwardly our own internal conscience and its consciousness, of which we are as yet only just aware? And however long it may take, and whatever "method" or "system" may be employed, is there not only one purpose in the whole relationship, namely that both evolve, so that as each is a growing point in the Universe, the Universe will evolve?

Is not a teacher someone who no longer needs reminding by another person to awaken and who keeps himself awake, as it were, in order to awaken others who wish to be wakened, and in turn, paradoxically, is awakened by an interchange of energy with the pupil? But for the relationship of the teacher and the pupil to have life must not both be fired by love of a mutual aim? How can two people relate unless there is a connecting force between them?

Although in passing time, in the world of appearances, one person has the role of teacher and is acknowledged as such, and another person has the role of the pupil, so that the teacher is respected as superior to the pupil and is expected to take responsibility for him, is it merely naive to accept such definitions of their roles when one has tasted, if only momentarily, a world where everything is connected, where there is no beginning and no ending, and everything is in its place? As we are in the world of appearances, in the world of passing time providing changing conditions but always postulating the same challenge, would it not merely be an attempt to disguise our present fragmented consciousness if we were to refuse to accept the standards of outward relationship between teacher and pupil? And if we refuse the outer world would the inner, latent, relationship ever be realized, so that we took the place of our teacher in the outer world and released him from recurrence? Does a pupil think enough, or at all, about his responsibility for his teacher?

If we excuse our present inability to awaken and remain awake because it is taught that we are awake, if only we knew it, are we not being so blind to our own insincerity that transformation of our being cannot occur? Is there not a strong probability, given our propensity to exaggerate the functions of the brain, that it is imagined that esoteric teaching can be understood by giving attention to reading, by listening to lectures and by use of any of the fashionable gadgets of "learning systems?" Given the necessity of informing a newcomer of the grounds of the subject he wishes to study, is it altogether wise to approach the study of esoteric teachings in the same way as subjects are studied in a university or in a technological college? Doesn't a student coming to learn a new perception of life totally different from the mentality engendered by upbringing need first to realize that his mind is hardly open at all to new ideas and that he cannot receive them if he demands to be taught on his own terms? Doesn't the teacher have to know how to break the shell surrounding a person, and the time when it is possible, so that the life locked within can emerge? And doesn't this method require the intimate surveillance of the pupil in order that his understanding may be germinated? How many pupils at a time can a teacher hold in mind?

If intimate surveillance, as part of a teaching method, is displaced in favor of large classes of pupils seldom receiving any individual notice, the teacher may be freed from possible, stupid adulation and the pupil may have to make greater effort to support himself, both of which things are healthy, but is something valuable lost? Are esoteric schools succumbing to the herd instinct, without realizing it, in which case their *raison d'être* has ceased, or are they adapting intelligently to the demands of a population so much larger than before?

In myth, symbol, legend and parable mankind's position on Earth and his relationship to a level of being higher than, and to a level of being lower than, his own is related: so obstinate and persistent is the repetition of this triple relationship of man—to himself and to two other levels of being–that it may be stale from over-familiarity. Or does it act as a reminder of what we always are but which is too deeply buried within us to be remembered and affect our daily lives? Doesn't this theme endure because of its vital importance to mankind? Haven't we the responsibility to realize its meaning and to see that it is available to the next generation? Can this be done with traditional words, however true is the good they enunciate? Hasn't the meaning to be realized by every generation and to be reformulated from generation to generation, to protect it from becoming petrified? And to convey the meaning, surely this needs frequent change of method, intelligent flexibility, understanding ideas on all levels of their meaning, so as to express it in a language that will penetrate current mechanical attitudes?

But was the relationship between all pupils and all teachers always intimate and private? Do we know if the teacher named in a particular scripture, for example, and his pupil are more than representations of a kind of relationship that is possible only at a certain psycho–logical stage between the two? Are we not too apt to jump to the conclusion that teachers are obliged to admit their pupils to their presence all the time and give them "special tuition?" Are we unaware that although teachers have responsibility to transmit their teachings and to make them available to those who take enough trouble to find them, they also have the responsibility of discerning who has ground within them good enough to bring forth good fruit, and who has only stony ground within them?

In benevolence to mankind teachings are broadcast as acorns from an oak tree. Only one oak may germinate from all the acorns shed each season, but others fertilize the ground in which it grows. To fertilize the stony ground of men's minds surely the organic manure of teachings needs to be plentiful and well ploughed in, so that there may be a crop of men and women in every generation to partake of conscious evolution?

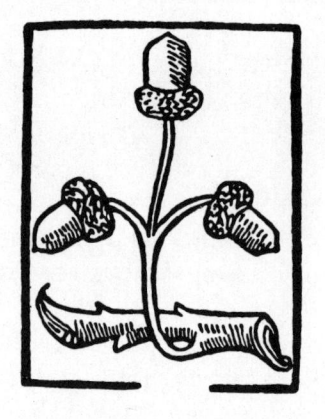

---

1. See the Bible, Matthew 13, or *The Mark* by Dr. Maurice Nicoll.

Relationship

Chögyam Trungpa

According to the Buddhist scriptures, a true guide is one who helps you to cross the turbulent river, then burns your boat for you.

VIEW BASED ON ETERNITY

Eternity is one of the notions we most cherish as an encouragement for our lives. We feel that since there is eternity, there will be eternal communication. Somehow or other there will be an endless continuity to give meaning to things, spiritual in nature or otherwise. Relationships can develop against this background in an atmosphere of transcendental promise.

We hardly realize how this attitude influences our approach towards relationships. "When I became good friends with somebody in high school, I automatically expected the friendship to go on forever. Fifteen years ago a buddy of mine and I built a cabin. Still we celebrate our comradeship by going over how skillfully we did the framing, the joints, what nails we used, etc." This is an eternal offering on the altar of our deathless friendship.

Many relationships are formed on the basis of some common pain or some task being shared. We tend to make a big deal of this pain or that task; we make it the keepsake of the relationship. Or else people meet in circumstances of lively common interest, where communication flows without obstacles. The usual procedure then is to celebrate the smoothness as if fending off a common enemy. Either way, the pain or the smoothness develops a legendary quality in regard to the relationship. Under such a sign, the relationship can be regarded as truly meaningful against its backdrop of eternity.

"Good friends" implies forever. You expect that the person you are committed to in that way will pour honey on your grave; otherwise you will feel you have been cheated. You are constantly struggling to keep your eternal friendship beautiful, which becomes an enormous strain on the relationship. Nevertheless, this is the model of relationship presented by the theistic tradition, such as the Christian or Hinduist. Having such a relationship is regarded as behaving as God commanded or as coming closer to the example of God's own love, which is eternal.

The idea of eternity has been misunderstood. It has been understood in a sense where eternity proves profundity rather than profundity proving eternity. We tend to assume that something is going to go on forever and therefore it is veneration towards a piece of rusty fence wire, known to have been hanging on a fence at a famous Civil War battle. We venerate it for its eternity rather than for its profundity. Ironically, it actually becomes a profound statement because of the basic truth of impermanence.

In societies influenced by a nontheistic point of view such as the Buddhist or Confucian, at the sophisticated level at least, relationship is more a matter of good manners and integrity than of approaching an eternal, divine model. There is less sense of guilt, but there is still a sense of righteousness or acting justly. In this humanistic context, relationship seems to be based on a model derived from ancient patterns of barter. In the commerce of barter, more was involved than just vying for monetary units. Something of value had to be given and something of value was received in exchange. Still a venerable model is involved.

View Derived from the Sense of Death

Distrust and suspicion of eternity or the venerable model arise. One has a sense of what might go wrong with the relationship, or what might go right for that matter, independent of one's will. There is a suggestion of inevitable chaos or death. Fearing the independent spontaneous development of relationship, one tries to ignore one's actual emotions and independent will. Brave people do this semi-consciously by developing a sense of mission or dogma in the relationship. Cowardly people manage it as a subconscious twist.

In general the brave strategy is less successful than the cowardly in creating an "ideal" relationship. It can only succeed by continually making its basically illogical position logically believable to the friend or partner. Then constant maintenance of the magnificent edifice is required. The less brave but more diligent do the whole work without ever confronting the partner on major issues. Instead he or she continually puts off the sense of death onto a thousand small things. The partner forgets to put the cap back on the ketchup bottle, always squeezes the toothpaste tube at the wrong end. The fault lies in all these little things.

In spite of philosophical and religious beliefs in eternity, there is a sense of the constant threat of death. The relationship is doomed. Whether cowardly or brave, you are trapped in no-alternatives, the actual situation, making constant patchwork to survive.

Disappearance of All View through Realizing that Death and Life Are One

Making a big deal out of relationship is deathly; as when, in chopping an onion, one becomes more conscious of the chopper than the chopping process. Quite possibly one might chop one's fingers off. When one begins to realize this, the sense of helplessness is startling. Viewpoint and attitude don't help. They are no more than a shell. The theistic view of a naive belief in eternity and the humanistic view of good manners and dignity are both merely conventional games remote from the actuality of the situation. Their adages of relationship, such as "patience is a virtue" or "death before dishonor" are not just the products of convention; they are in themselves purely conventional.

The idea of relationship needs to fall apart. When one realizes that life is the expression of death and death is the expression of life, that continuity cannot exist without discontinuity, then there is no longer any need to cling to one and fear the other. There is no longer any ground for the brave or the cowardly. One sees that the relationship is the lack of any viewpoint whatsoever.

One might think that such relationship is only for the spiritually advanced, but actually it is just normal and ordinary. Any conceptual reference point becomes destructive. One actually begins to believe that the relationship does not exist. But there is no need to worry: the non-existence of the relationship is continually a powerful breeding ground of relationship. Whereas a covenant of trust breeds further mistrust, wariness of trust can bring an enormously warm relationship.

This wariness is still a viewpoint, but it is one that is open to surprises, unlike living in the promise of a philosophical view. It is also unlike complete mistrust, a viewpoint which does not allow the naiveté of relationship to flower.

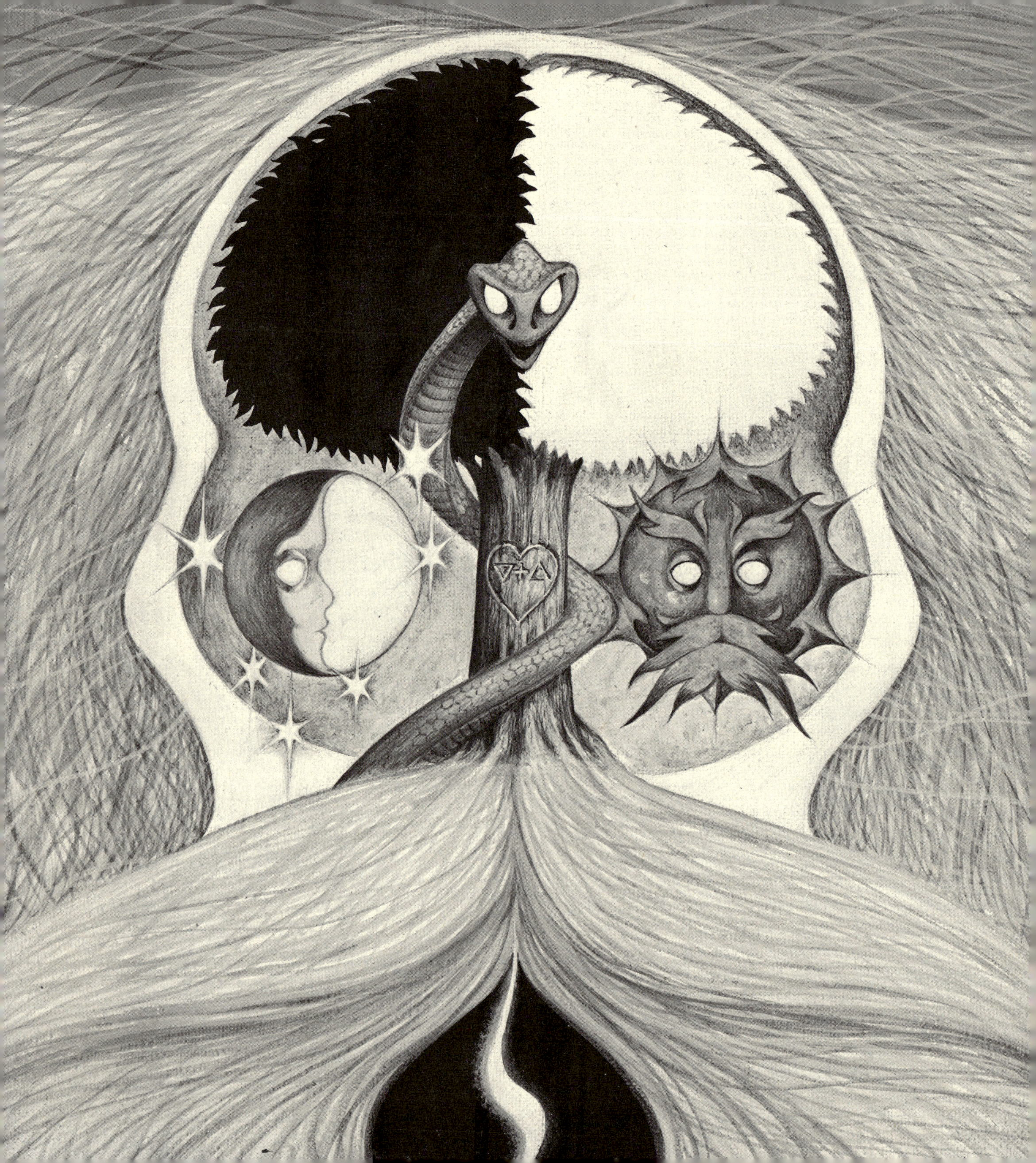

An Alchemical Allegory:
Notes Towards an Understanding of Genesis

Charles Poncé

*Batter my heart, three personed God, for you
As yet but knock, breathe, shine, and seek to mend
That I may rise and stand, o'erthrow me and bend
Your force to break, blow, burn and make me new.*

John Donne

For this reason a man shall leave his father and his mother and be joined to his wife, and the two shall become one flesh.

Mark, 10:7-9

To the Reader: The following is but a preliminary attempt to understand the meaning of a myth central to the psychology of our cultural background. Some of the proposals set forth may appear blasphemous, but to this commentator the greater blasphemy is the silence that has surrounded the questions that the myth poses. It is with this thought in mind that this small allegory is offered.

HERMAPHRODISM AND THE FRUIT OF SIN

The tale of Genesis is too well known to be repeated in its entirety. The important features necessary for our discussion are as follows:

1. God creates Adam in His own image.
2. He forbids him to eat of the Tree of the Knowledge of Good and Evil lest he die.
3. He creates Eve from a rib in Adam's side.
4. The serpent induces Eve to eat of the Tree and convince Adam that he should also.
5. Immediately upon eating of the Tree both their eyes are opened and they perceive each other's nakedness.
6. God discovers the 'sin' and banishes the two to the desert outside of Paradise.

There are many who will insist that this is a superficial outline of a tale replete with hidden meanings, and they would be right in that none of these meanings are on the surface of the tale. It is precisely because the *surface* of the tale has influenced our culture that we shall ignore these subtler meanings. It is sometimes necessary when discussing such material to suffer the embarrassment of naked exposition, remembering all the while that it is a natural tendency to look for the hidden while overlooking the obvious.

The first symbol to be considered is that of the hermaphroditic Adam. The hermaphrodite, in general, must be recognized as a symbolic expression of two different types of psychic orientation or consciousness, the masculine portion representing all that may be identified with the masculine, the feminine with all that which may be identified with the feminine. And here we are faced with a problem, for each culture imposes certain of its own deficiencies and expectations into the definitions of these polarities. An apparent instance of this may be found in the general attitude that the feminine is the more inferior and weaker of the two; a less apparent instance, coming from contemporary quarters where the value of the feminine is undergoing rejuvenation, that the masculine is self-centered and tyrannical. We must in our inquiry temporarily put aside any discussion of what may or may not be the true "qualities" of the masculine and the feminine and instead address ourselves solely to the fact of their polarity. It is not our place here to discuss sexuality *per se*, but rather to discuss the symbolism of the hermaphrodite which is basically asexual.

The figure of the hermaphrodite has been traditionally employed in the language of symbolism to demarcate the beginning and end of a process. As symbolic of a beginning state the figure most familiar to us in the West is that of the original Adam containing his wife within his chest. The Jewish branch of mysticism known as Kabbalism recognized the implications of this symbolism and took it to also symbolize the end of their mystical quest. To their way of thinking every man is both masculine and feminine. The Sefirothic system as paradigmatic of the human body is an apt depiction of this idea. The Christian European alchemist was in basic agreement with this Kabbalistic view, the only difference being that the hermaphroditic figure standing at the end of their process was the Christ in the form of the Philosopher's Stone. What is curious is that both Judaism and Christianity also begin with and accept the figure of the hermaphrodite but neither of them hold the figure up as symbolic of a religious life. In each instance it was necessary that the renegade factor, the mystics and philosophers working outside of the mainstream of traditional religious belief, reveal the nature of the end process in these terms. The difference between the first and second representations of the hermaphrodite in a process lies in the idea that the latter figure represents a unity that has come about through the agency of a transformative experience—one that has caused the polarities therein to perceive one another, suffer each other's differences, and reconcile their divergent natures under the auspices of love.

The opposites in their original hermaphroditic state symbolize a condition of unconsciousness wherein they reside in blissful ignorance of one another. This original status also occurs, or is implied, in those world mythologies where we are told that the anthropomorphic figures of heaven and earth as father and mother existed in an undivided state; so too in mystical theologies where the polarities expressive of the human condition are illustrated as entwined or enmeshed with one another: the Kundalini entwined around the lingam in Tantric yoga and the yin and yang as exemplary of two modes of action enmeshed in the figure of the T'ai Chi of Chinese philosophy. In each instance, the implication is that the hermaphroditic figure is either symbolic of the total unity of God, or God Himself.

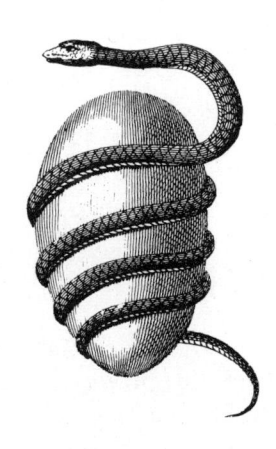

When the God of Genesis "and all the host of heaven standing beside him on his right hand and on his left," (I Kings 22:19) said "Let us make man in our image, after our likeness" (Genesis 1:26), He too created a hermaphroditic figure modeled after Himself. However, the admonition given this newborn creature not to eat of the Tree of the Knowledge of Good and Evil implies that he is not a true image. At the most, the creature's awareness is limited to a process of naming (... "and whatever the man called every living creature, that was its name." Genesis 2:19) similar to that encountered in a young infant.

The radical alteration of God's image by His own hand that occurs when God extracts Eve from the body of Adam represents the first act of differentiation that occurs within the infantile psyche. Here, the first step away from the unconscious hermaphrodite is taken with the appearance of two distinct units or opposites. But with this first act of differentiation a strange event occurs. The division of the figures yields a type of creature God had not anticipated. Here for the first time the *possibility* of consciousness occurs. And that possibility comes to full fruition when Eve is induced by the Serpent to eat of the Tree and convince Adam to follow suit.

Then the eyes of both were opened, and they knew that they were naked, and they sewed fig leaves together and made themselves aprons (Genesis 3:7)

Here, suddenly, for the first time since their separation out of the original hermaphroditic mold modeled after their Maker the two *perceive* one another. They look at each other and see each other in their nakedness; they have feeling for one another. They have become Gods in that they are capable of perceiving the opposites, and it is this ability that abruptly separates them from the lower order of creatures, that makes them not only unique, but in part divine. For the divinity of being is consciousness, and consciousness is the one sin that we all commit when we move away from the commandments of the paradisical lassitude of our unconscious natures. It is for this first act of disobedience against that which would keep us as children, blind to the reality that everywhere touches us, that the gates of Paradise become barred. So too in the maturing child does there come a time when the free-floating pleasures of childhood suddenly end, the young ego seemingly being cast out forever into the harsh and unsupportive desert of consciousness.

The harshness of the young ego's first encounter with all that exists outside of the paradisical unconscious is nowhere better illustrated than in the Apocryphal book entitled *The Book of Adam and Eve* where we are told of Adam's several attempts at suicide immediately upon being cast out of Eden. Adam's predicament is a simple one: he is suddenly subject to the hardships of being-in-the-world, witness to the burden of consciousness that the ego must heroically take up to successfully accomplish the transition from the paradise of a childhood free of conflict, to the reality of the opposites of which our world is composed. It is this willingness to take upon oneself the conflict of the opposites that exist beyond the gates of Paradise that gives birth to the transformative experience of suffering to which the serpent awakens the first couple.

What we have in the figure of Adam is the picture of the germinal ego coming into being in the pleroma of the unconscious. That the Adam of Paradise represents what will become the ego is implied in the fact that he is made in the image of God, and that as God rules over the paradise of the unconscious, Adam too will one day rule over the desert of consciousness existing beyond the Gates of Paradise. In short, the ego that rules consciousness is but the image of God, or the Self, that rules the unconscious. The differentiation of this ego begins while it is still within the gates of the unconscious and is symbolized by the extraction of the feminine principle which we are told is of the essence of bone. That is, the feminine on the way to becoming has its origin in that which many religions symbolically identify with the eternal and divine. Even in our culture the skeleton stands for that which remains after death as symbolic of the barrier existing between the transpersonal and the mundane, between being and non-being. Both primitive and more advanced cultures employ different portions of the skeleton as *mana* objects, treating them as they would divinity itself. In addition, this feminine figure is taken from that portion of Adam's body closest to the heart—the place traditionally identified with emotion and intuitive knowledge. Eve, therefore, in that she is a portion of what is at once hidden but supportive, eternal and divine, wisdom-inducing and passionate, symbolizes a component of our psyches that is at once immortal and human; that mediates between being and non-being. In short Eve represents the soul.

Universally it is the soul's function to mediate between the world of mankind and the divine; she is often described as the bearer of messages in the form of dreams and visions—in other words she operates through the realm of symbols. It is in this sense that the soul might be thought of as that which mediates between the conscious and unconscious portions of our psyches. We have also suggested that it is because of the inquisitiveness of this soul principle that consciousness is won from the unconscious, that it is Eve who leads Adam to the fruit of the Tree. This too, traditionally, is yet another function of the soul: to inform, to direct, to guide, and to cause enlightenment. With this act of defiance the true separation from the unconscious takes place. The ego becomes locked out of Paradise, the soul going with it into the desert, her connectedness to the divine serving as the only link between the transpersonal and the mundane. Again, the idea of the feminine soul exiled from the divine and trapped on earth is also a common theme in mythology and world religion.

Between the initial state of the hermaphrodite symbolic of the unconscious union of the opposites and the final state of the hermaphrodite symbolic of the marriage of all opposites in consciousness, there then appear the stages of life comprised of the conflict of the opposites.

THE WISDOM OF THE SERPENT
"Now the serpent was more subtle than any other wild creature that the Lord God had made." (Genesis 3:25). That the serpent is "more subtle" is a major understatement. Here was the sole creature in the Garden not

only capable of speech, but also knowing that God was lying to Adam when He told him that the fruit of the tree would cause death. The serpent tells Eve she need not fear the tree:

> *You will not die. For God knows that when you eat of it your eyes will be opened and you will be like God, knowing Good and Evil.* (Genesis 3: 4, 5)

The serpent is a cold-blooded creature who in at least one system of transformation (Kundalini yoga) has been identified with the sympathetic nervous system; that is, identified with the so-called autonomous portion of our being. Because the serpent symbolizes transformation through its activity of skin-shedding, and because it knows the true results of what will happen when the fruit of the Tree of the Knowledge of Good and Evil is eaten, we must assume that it represents yet another form of consciousness. Considering the serpent and his relation to the first couple, it obviously represents the consciousness of the psychic system that comes into being when the human organism becomes a reality. It is, in other words, the inborn instinctual wisdom that God had not reckoned on, the spirit in nature that complements the spirit of God hovering above the waters of Creation. In the same manner that God is complemented by the figure of Adam, so too is the spirit of God complemented by the spirit in nature. This is the core of what is unique in humanity: it contains a spirit that is diametrically opposed to the spirit of God who originally desired the perfection and stability of a Paradise. The spirit of nature, on the other hand, demands of us imperfection and change for without these two states the need for and experience of transformation does not occur. And this is something that God Himself had no knowledge of originally: transformation. He was complete in Himself, without imperfection. The serpent in psychological terms may be thought of as the cold-blooded range of instincts through which we experience transformation. Thus transformation comes to us through the instinctual range of our experience, through the first-hand experience of our autonomous nature.

All of which leads us to an important question: What is the serpent in relation to God? How is it that of all the creatures in the Garden it alone was capable of knowing God's most secret thoughts; what is it about this creature that allows it to know the true secret of the tree, that allows it to know what even God Himself appears to be ignorant of—that the creature Eve carries within her the seed of consciousness in the form of curiosity and that questions about the unknown are a temptation to her? Here we are obviously faced with a consciousness equal to God's in that it not only knows the past, the true value of the tree, the psychic disposition of Eve, but also has some inkling of the potentialities inherent in the entire situation. We can only conclude from these facts that the serpent is symbolic of an aspect of God Himself, that its almost God-like consciousness is just that—a split off portion of God's psyche.

The Dream of God

Now we must consider the phenomenon of Genesis from God's viewpoint investigating the possible reasons for His committing Himself to the act. Throughout Genesis, up to the creation of the hermaphroditic Adam, God goes about the entire matter of Creation in a rather straight forward manner. We gain little insight into His psychology or His feelings until the day when He says to Himself:

> *It is not good that the man should be alone; I will make him a helper fit for him.*
> (Genesis 2:18)

In this statement we have a clue to the reason why the project of Creation was ever undertaken, for God's ability to empathize with another's loneliness could only have grown out of a first-hand experience. There are a number of world mythologies that tell us the Creation of the universe grew out of the Creator's experience of loneliness and the ensuing desire to create something that he can relate to. A fine example is given us in the Winnebago Creation myth.

> *What it was our father lay on when he came to consciousness we do not know ... He began to think of what he should do and finally began to cry ... He said, 'As things are just as I wish them I shall make one being like myself.' So he took a piece of earth and made it like himself. Then he talked to what he had created but it did not answer. He looked upon it and he saw that it had no mind or thought. So he made a mind for it. Again he talked to it, but it did not answer ... So he looked upon it again and saw that it had no soul. So he made it a soul. He talked to it again and it very nearly said something. But it did not make itself intelligible. So Earthmaker breathed into its mouth and talked to it and it answered.*

Again, in the *Satapatha Brahmana* we are told that the soul of the universe, Purusha, was alone. Hence,

> *He did not enjoy happiness. He desired a second. He caused this same self to fall asunder into two parts. Thence there arose a husband and wife. From them men were born.*

The striking similarity between the Winnebago tale and Genesis, right down to the creation of an Eve-soul for the creature and the imparting of breath by Earthmaker to animate his creature is apparent. Our example from Hindu mythology also complements Genesis in that the Creator himself is a hermaphroditic creature whose division gives birth to the first couple. In Genesis, God does not perform this operation on Himself but instead creates a creature in His own image in much the same manner that the Winnebago God does. In both these instances, as in others too long to relate here, the creation begins because of God's experience of loneliness. In our Western tale, God does not start straight off with the creation of a divine couple but, as in the Winnebago tale (not included in the excerpt), sets about the creation of the world proper. The experience of loneliness, these tales appear to be telling us, can be a creative experience if handled properly. That is, the experience if turned inwards unites one with unknown aspects of one's own personality—in this instance, one's creative abilities. Ultimately, loneliness is a yearning for something or someone representative or symbolic of an interior component of ourselves that either longs to be united with us, or that we long to be united with. Expressed psychologically, this yearning is for something that is not known to us consciously, that is hidden deep within the unconscious portions of our psyches. We humans are afforded the opportunity to gain access to the hidden portions of ourselves through the agency of symbols that appear in either dreams, visions, or through methods that call forth the imaginative faculty of the unconscious. The latter constitute disciplined meditational techniques or a type of purposefully directed play that allows the unconscious to display itself during the waking state. Jung called this latter method (active imagination) a short-cut method to the unconscious, its purpose being to allow the unconscious immediate access to consciousness, and *vice versa*.

Because in the tale of Genesis, as well as in the two examples taken from other sources, the act of Creation grows out of a conscious decision on the part of God ("Let us make..."), we would here suggest that the Creation took place through such an experiment in imagination. In an attempt to discover the hidden aspect of Himself with which He wished to be united, God allowed His unconscious to create an image of the material attempting to come into the light of consciousness. In much the same manner that the unconscious in human beings creates dreams as reflective of our hidden nature, so too did God spin out of His unconscious that aspect of His hidden nature with which He was not reconciled. Whereas our unconscious lives are ephemeral and without material substance, His unconscious life took on substance. His images were to have as much life as the images we find in our dreams; His images were to live themselves forward regardless of His commandments in much the same manner that the process of our unconscious lives live themselves forward regardless of our conscious and rational commands. The creation of a creature in His own image constituted an attempt at introspection, an attempt to "get a look" at Himself, as it were. The hermaphroditic Adam would therefore be symbolic of the unknown and hidden value that was attempting to become united with His consciousness. In other words, Adam symbolized the proverbial fly in the ointment, the unknown portion of God's psyche that constituted His blind spot.

The figure of Adam symbolizes the problem concealed in God's psyche; humanity in turn represents the psychoanalytic process that God undergoes by committing Himself to an act of creative imagination. The pain and conflict that we undergo in our attempts at self-awareness is but symbolic of the same process God undergoes through the history of the human race. We are the conflict, the pain, the confusion of His own transformation.

History is God's self-analysis. We are His dream over which He has as little control as we do ours. In order for us to in any way creatively and positively affect the nature of our dream lives we must first arrive at a proper conscious standpoint in our relationship with the unconscious. So too, we must assume, must God act toward his "unconscious," the sphere of which is the created world, if He is to realize the dark and unknown aspect of his own personality symbolized by the serpent. All of which now brings us to the question of what God might have been unconscious of to begin with.

The Serpent on the Cross

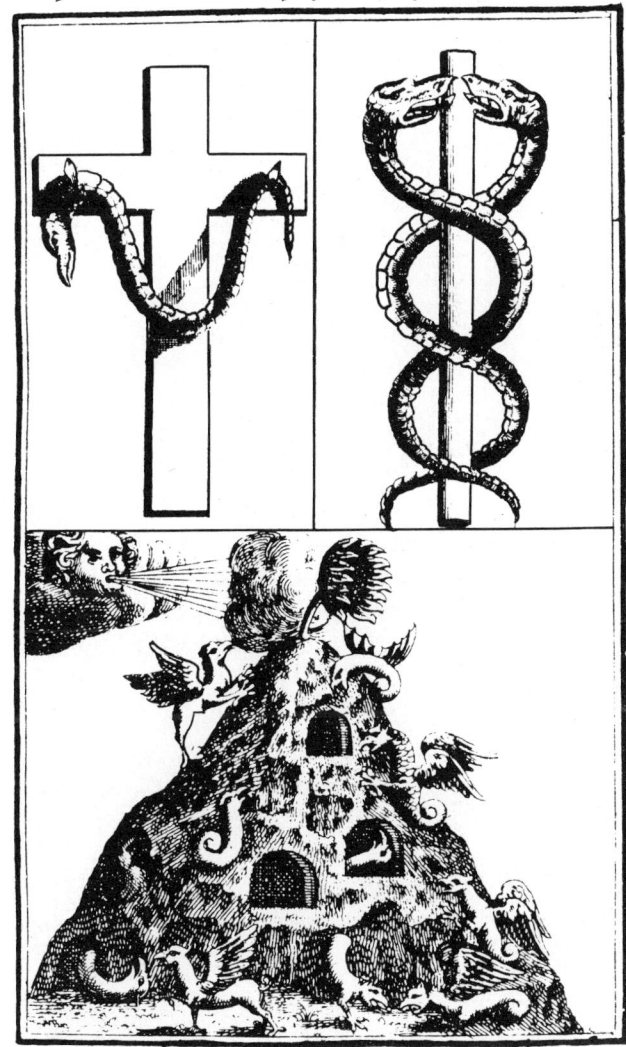

The experience of loneliness, the yearning for the unknown and unseen within us, the thing scratching at our dreams, can, if not properly attended to, lead us into states of inexplicable outbursts of emotion, fear, and particularly rage. Invariably, one ends up vacillating between the experience of extreme emotion and boredom. As Paul Tillich once correctly surmised, boredom is rage spread thin. The phenomenon of rage presents us with a peculiar ambiguity. On the one hand, a person overcome with rage usually appears to be acting out of a passionate emotion, in the "heat of anger" as it is usually referred to. On the other hand the results of such a state are actually unfeeling acts. Hidden within this so-called heat of anger is a cold-blooded instinctual response to situations that the individual for some reason or other finds untenable. One aspect of the symbolism of the serpent in the tale of Genesis is just this type of cold-bloodedness. In the light of the frequent outbursts of rage that the Old Testament God often displays, we would suggest here that the serpent (which we have described as a split-off portion of God's psyche) symbolizes the cold-blooded and instinctual side of God's unrealized problem. The fact that God is not aware of the knowledge that the serpent contains, the fact that he overlooks its presence in the Garden of his imagination, indicates that He is not only blind to this rage, but that He has actually repressed it out of sight. In that the serpent is also symbolic of transformative powers and consciousness, the secret of God's problem is to be discovered in the very thing that He rejects. However, rage and cold-bloodedness, loneliness and boredom are only symptoms. The serpent is but the energic principle of the unrealized problem symbolized by the hermaphroditic Adam. The problem is to be found in God's unity.

What the image of Himself reveals to God is the fact that the unity He represents is composed of opposites. Because God, not only in our tradition but in every tradition known to us, is defined as a unity of opposites, the one thing that He cannot know of is the experience of the opposites in a divided state. God has the *knowledge* of the opposites, but not the *experience* of their effects. He has only experienced the peaceful unity of the opposites. The knowledge that He has of them constitutes a philosophical assumption. In order to experience the true effects of the opposites He must first divide them. This is the nature of God's blind spot in Genesis, the source of his rage in the Old Testament—this little piece of unconsciousness concerning an aspect of His psyche of which He has had no experience.

So, the whole of Genesis from the beginning up to the expulsion is symbolized throughout by division. With the division of the hermaphroditic Adam into male and female the process of self-awareness begins. However, as is more often than not the case, this first attempt to take a look at Himself fails for He assumes (as we so often also do) that He knows exactly what He looks like, knows without a doubt all of the components of His personality. Adam, however, is a pure intellectual construction for he is made up of those things that God chooses as being relevant for his creation. The active and motivating principle of His problem, the energy necessary for transformation symbolized by the serpent, is repressed, overlooked, lurking in the shadows. Adam as symbolic of God's problem is an intellectualization similar to those lists we often compose as illustrative of our good and bad qualities. God does not really want to consider the moral problems posed by His knowledge of Good and Evil, hence He leaves those qualities out of the image He would employ as an introspective aid. But the unconscious will not allow Him to escape the issue. The repressed value intrudes itself and sets up a situation in which the moral issue He does not want to consider is presented to Him in a symbolic play. It shows Him that the repressed value contains transformative energies and a consciousness of its own; that to achieve consciousness and discover the nature of one's own inferiority it is at times necessary to go against one's own ego-dominated commandments. In this regard, the serpent symbolizes the innate wisdom of the instinctual portion of the psyche to heal and transform itself. It attempts to reveal this fact to God, but instead of pausing long enough to consider that the mishap came about because of an error in His judgment, He elects to pass the blame on. The suffering that would have arisen by His wrestling with the problems in the issue of Good and Evil is instead heaped on the shoulders of His creation. In other words, He represses the problem even further.

What the serpent attempted to show God on the stage of Paradise was that transformation can only be experienced by a willingness to take on the suffering implicit in any act of becoming conscious; that to gain access to an unrealized portion of His own being, God would have to experience the conflict of the opposites at first hand. To achieve this He would have to commit Himself totally to the experiment. The task would have been easier if He had dealt with it within the confines of His carefully constructed vessel called Paradise. Having failed in that experiment, He would have to follow the lead that the psyche imposed upon Him. He would have to experience the conflict *in* the world, which in His reality meant that he would have to make a total descent into His unconscious. In short, He would have to become mortal in the figure of the Christ in order to experience the conflict peculiar to humanity. It would only be there, on the Cross, in that mass of nerve and muscle, that God could experience what was unknown to Him: the conflict inherent in the disunity that expresses itself in suffering. It was only in this manner that the symptom of His unconsciousness could be transformed. It was there where the serpent of His psyche would in time be experienced firsthand by that manifestation of Himself in the form of the Christ who would himself say, during a discussion on the necessity of being reborn:

And as Moses lifted up the serpent in the wilderness, so must the Son of man be lifted up, that whoever believes in him may have eternal life. (John 3:14,15)

And in such a manner was God to eventually resolve his psychic difficulty. From a wrathful, vengeful, and unpredictable despot He was to be transformed into a God of Love through the agency of our humanity. It is through this act of transformation that the hermaphrodite appears again in the person of Christ who by his traditional identification with the Second Adam becomes associated with the hermaphroditism which began the process.

The Christ therefore symbolizes the suffering inherent in the fusion of the divine with the human portions of our psyches. That is, it is at that point where we suffer the greatest anguish in the desert of this world to which we have been exiled that we may know we are contributing to the self-realization of God Himself. It is only during such moments in the Work that we may fully know we are in the presence of the transpersonal.

———

And in all this there is concealed the meaning of the statement that the Stone is the Christ and that the stages of the Work are revealed to us in the seven days of Creation. By this it is to be understood that God's task was that of separating the opposites so that He could experience their differences; and that our task is that of uniting the opposites so that we might have knowledge of their unity, which is God.

This is the meaning of the marriage of the sun and moon, of the solar and lunar consciousness we have been allotted, and without whose union we deny God the experience of Himself.

Relationship: The Ship of Fools

Ruth Hoebel

Relationship is irrational; it is opposed to a kind of objectivity that separates things, entities and concepts. This objectivity is commonly known as Rationality: it separates and classifies, it defines and concretizes all things. Relationship, being irrational, moves and merges, changing the definitions of things and people constantly. Relationship is Love and Life and so cannot be defined. In speaking of it we can never satisfy those who long for the concrete, the final definition, the resting place; in speaking of it we must be irrational.

Eros is the god of Love but more abstractly he is relatedness, he is the gravity that attracts all objects to one another. He is the strange whimsical and savage Pan that connects us all from our bellies and our sex, from our hearts and our minds irrevocably. Whatever dramas occur in the rational world of businesses, marriages, castes and hierarchies, these irrational connections still exist, and go on affecting us profoundly from the irrational side, from the night side or the unconscious.

This relatedness is universal, connecting plants, minerals, humans, animals and stars. The poet feels this connection quite a lot more than the rest of us. Dylan Thomas makes us feel myriads of homely human and natural things in their complex relatedness. The rhythm of his song makes our blood and tissue, our ancestral longings, our hair, our roots reach out and connect with the landscape and the people of his Welsh rural life experience, or rather I should say it calls up impossible memories of a secret landscape of our own which is universal.

To speak of Relationship is to speak in paradox. It is always a paradox. What we yearn for in the other is in ourselves but being universal it is in the other as well, because there is no separation in the realm of the irrational where we dwell much more than we imagine. We are the same and not the same. I know just what you mean no matter what you say but I do not always choose to know it. Remain a mystery, illusive, carry me away to gardens where I will meet myself.

But this is not to say that Love is iconoclasm or narcissism either. Amongst our many relationships, our relationship with everything, the bond links us with ourselves. A flower for example, or a crystal or excrement is the perfect mirror of our selves, of our Self. The Self is the enigma; it is the whole of all these connected objects in the world, in the worlds. We may seek the Self as if it were our own, but it is never experienced that way. Our sense of exclusiveness, of ownership on any level leaves as we approach the Self. The Self is unknowable only because there is no one there at the moment of truth to know it. One is overwhelmed by the universality, by the structure of the world crumbling, by avenues of possibility casting seeds in infinite directions. One is overwhelmed by freedoms that sat on the doorstep and out on the fire-escape for a thousand years.

And returning from a taste of infinity we find a different world. Are we really mad if we now talk to cats and flowers, are offended by boxcars and supermarkets? Dylan Thomas' song is weaving everything together, the rusty bolts and coolaid stands, the hyacinths and a friend who is walking quickly over his memories, following them through shade and sunlight both. Now we dip into another's eyes and see our face very small reflected back and it looks very unnameable there, beautiful perhaps framed in the face, in the eye, in the iris of the eye of the other.

In relationship there is the other, the Other. He or she or it are mirrors, mirrors, mirrors, like a room of mirrors, right angle mirrors reflecting our image into infinity but differently at each point. When the Other is the most other that is when we begin to see our Self reflected more truly. The mystery that makes us gasp and say "You are so other," in a whisper to the Other, makes us feel so close that we begin to merge, at the same time merging with everything. The high tempo of Dylan Thomas' poetics reverberates, Blake's holy sensuality and acuity emerge. A ship comes, the Ship of Fools, where rules do not apply. This ship flies on the sea of irrationality, no land will let it moor. Sensory deprivation is the price of civilization. On the Ship of Fools the Infant is king again; there is touching and kissing, tears, fears, fights, flights, there is something broader than human rights, there are Being rights, the right to be in the moment.

When we return from the Ship of Fools we see relationship quite differently. Knowing that anything is possible makes many more things possible where rules seem to reign. So we begin the subtle experiment of "playing with that which plays with us." We can love the most unlikely people, cross class and archetypal boundaries, love parts of ourselves we have always hated, bring buried feelings to the surface. We can experiment and play knowing that the rules are arbitrary. The Self is myriad formed, all creatures stick to it, its facets capture everything. We can laugh now where we cried before, cry where we laughed, because the rigid social forms have become transparent and we can see the soul of everything. The meaning of human relationship is not to bind another to ourselves but to discover what the real connection is, to travel a somewhat tortuous, dangerous perhaps, labyrinthine path to this end. We need to unbind the instincts in order to tame them with Love rather than break them with unbearable repression.

To be the Fool is the most difficult thing of all for a civilized person to be, yet this is just what one needs to be released. To dance, to sing, to laugh, to play the Fool is to be naked, to be the beast, the babe at the breast of Life's chaotic overabundance. The Fool is close to the Self, it takes whatever comes, weeps at tragedy, laughs full and loud at the wonderful, never puts on a false face to disguise its feelings, never plays the games that would lead to such a ploy. The Fool mimics others. Mime is the Fool's favorite game, to say with all the gestures of stilted societies' most usual poses that is after all only a game.

The heart is the Fool, in its innocence it does not discriminate, all are equal in its tender vocation. The heart is not maudlin nor nostalgic; it lives in the moment like the savage and breathes fire. Next to Love all things are diminished. All the ego's investments, all the penitences of conditioning, all the recriminations of social justice tumble like stage sets. Eros enters and beguiles, his ancient eyes reflect only the truth. His flame burns up the dross of every accumulation. Eros walks at nightfall through lush green grasses, his feet are wet in the dew but never cold. All our eyes are upon him, when we sleep and when we love, even when we hate. We dream we wished his curse would burn the tips of our fingers, the tips of our tongue, our eyelashes only and not consume us. We dream his curse utterly consumes us. The Other is our vocation. In relationship we find our thread which was perhaps lost an eon ago in the womb or the cradle or some other unfortunate place. Finding the footprints of our own lost track, the railroad track that ascends from the desert to the mountains, to forests, valleys and sensuous jungles. We leave the barrenness of the plains, of surfaces without inhabitants, of dimensions without end of loneliness. Loneliness is backtracking and hopping forward, never resting, never drinking from the river in eyes, never grazing in the mirrors in eyes that laugh and cry, that feel the sharp arrow of eternity wedged between lips that suck in breath that nourishes the sky. Loneliness is never to kiss oneself in the lips of another, never giving over the prized possession: one's "I am the Queen of Eternity," or "I am the demon of twelve thousand eyes."

*

Quickly licking up the flames of Eros, the flames of Eternity really, those long sunset planes of the moment of heirosgamos, licking up these flames, consuming oneself and the Other, we meet. I saw you see me. You saw me see you see me. I saw you see me see you. We laughed. The sky reverberated with laughter. We laughed. What else could we do? We made love. This was laughter too.

From now on when I see you we will make love somehow, as birds in bird's nest soup, with our eyelashes, with our friends' laughter, with their smiles, with their lovemaking. From now on when I see you I will remember who I am.

I came here tonight hoping to meet you and caught your eye in my sleeve. I plagiarized your smile, what brighter compliment could I pay you. You dreamed of me often before ever having seen my face. My wonderful face slid past you in the dream foliage and on seeing me, you vaguely remembered that face, "seen it before, how strangely it reflects a facet of my half known soul, a part a little in flame, a little in lightning flashes and aquarium meadows. Is it I who am queen of this soul or is it she?"

I passed you on the street hoping to remember you the same as before but your sameness is always different. This time you sent me whirling away like a spiral of dust and your eyes kept echoing after me. We hugged without touching, I still feel the warmth. Your smile has become part of my left shoulder blade.

I dreamed you were rotting but really it was me. When I was reborn a white flower with blue and violet center deep to look down in, you were amazingly different too. You are the mirror of my unknowns. I used to dump my garbage out the window into your garden imagining you were evil and this way I would do you good harm. Now fantastic flowers and magnificent trees grow there. See how we have cultivated a fine enemyship.

I dreamed you were my mother even though that is impossible. I dreamed of you for all these years and one day found your heart bleeding on my front room rug. It sang to me from severed depths, broken bridges, deserts of annihilation, its feet wounded like the knees of pilgrims at the Cathedral of Gaudelupe. Turning it over in my mind I saw your journey was like mine. To come so far for what is overabundant all around everywhere and nowhere. I saw a dance forming between us, a lovemaking without torsos, with memories of calypso cocktail waitresses and the Queen of Performances, the Prince of the center of attention, of simply wanting to be seen, of simply wanting to see oneself. Nobody knows me not even eye, not even I. Can you see me, am I here, who am I, what does it mean? These are the questions that send one whirling off in crazy directions away from others, away from the center, away from the self.

You saw me in my disguise; it slipped and you entered, hungry to see if I was really there to see you see yourself reflected in the mirror that I am. I saw you see your delight for just one moment and we clouded over with fright. But you know the way in and I know the way out, so tentatively we seek each other. I dreamed we were on stage singing a duet, changing and exchanging roles so quickly that the audience disappeared. We collapsed from exhaustion, our arms around each other, akimbo on the floor, at rest at last, the audience was gone. Who were they anyway?

The King of Everything Profound shook

his head and ran away down a street inside his eyes lined with trees of every kind. From out of the trees leaped nymphs and nymphets, and the Queen of May leading a gaggle of geese each on a ribbon of a different color. They laughed at him because the trap door in the seat of his pants hung down and a yellow mongrel dog was snapping at his ass. "Don't you know, my good man," said the Queen of Hearts, "that you are really the Fool?" "Oh," he said, "I nearly forgot," fondled the dog and came back saying he loved me.

Once there was the Prince of No Good. The price he paid seemed very small but the farther he traveled the more the price became. One day he lost his sheep's horn and his cloak of rainbows on one side and the starry night sky on the other. He wandered in a whirlwind where all his memories visited him like ghosts, they whispered that he was a dead man and lived for nothing, because he lived for no one not even himself. He lived only for a shred of darkness which was his mother's hair into which he crept to sleep at night and to hide. There he dreamed a life but never lived one. He fell off a precipice into the arms of a voluptuous woman and escaped into her hair, he rested there like an ornament disguised as a butterfly. The Queen of Hearts came one day and demanded payment. "Love, or your life" she said holding a sixgun to his heart. He tried to fly away on wings of feathers, on insect wings, on wings of platinum, silver and gold. So she shot him in the heart and all the remorses fled the wound as he grew pale as snow. Resurrected in the morning he found the words "I am Just" signed Eros tattooed upon his heart.

In the end there is nothing but possibilities within possibilities. The concrete reality of the Soul is fluid and constantly changing. The dreamer and the lover are masters of this realm. The Heart in its secret chambers is the ruler of this realm. Where the heart walks the commonplace is given special colors, angelic music and a peculiar radiance. This is the heaven on earth the poets speak of and the saints proclaim.

35

Love Song of the Loba

Diane di Prima

O my lord, blue beast
on the pale green snows, see
I have been running to keep up
w/you
        I have been
                  running to find you
my tongue
        scours ice your
                  tracks made
I drink
      hollows of yr steps,
                I thought
many a dark beast was you only to find
perfume of your fur, bright cloud
of yr breath not there, they are
flesh & clay, heavy dross, they do not
fly
   in the wind,
              see I have flown
to you, do you
        lurk in night
               do you sail
to sea on an ice floe
            howling sacred songs

O my lord, my good
     dark beast
        how is it
I cannot taste you
     wraith & shadow
tripleheaded
    blind god of my
        spirit, you burn
blue flame on the
     green ice, long shadows
lick at yr eyes
    yr fur like arctic night
        the fire
of your song

      I will circle the earth,
        I will circle the
          wheeling stars
     keening, my blue gems
        shoot signals
          to yr heart:
I am yr loved one, lost from eternity
         I am
   yr sakti
     wheeling thru
       black space
   I, the white wolf,
      Loba,
       call to you
   blue mate,
     O lost lord
       of the failing hills

The Loba Continues to Sing

I will make you flesh again
(have you slipped away)
think you to elude, become past
& black & white
as photographs,
     O I will
lure you into being till you stand
flesh solid against my own
     I will spread my hair
over yr slender feet
    my tongue
shall give you shape, I will
make you flesh & carry you
away, O bright
black lord you are, & I
your sister
    & magic carpet

Will you ride?

    ★

O I tumbled here for you, I put on flesh
drew down this skull over my flaming light
    slipped on this shaggy pelt
to make it easy for yr spirit to speak to mine

As in that bright unclouded ocean where the stars
are not yet born, where you & I
slid, tumbling like dolphins
      we cd not
speak each other's names,

    O you leaped
into the worlds, & I followed
did I not
   falling and shrieking
I solidified.
    Merely to look, my lord
once more
into your great
    sad beast eyes

Share this sorrow.

The Teacher and the Student

Herbert V. Guenther

It is rather a trite comment on the present situation to say that we live at a time when our values and goals are in a state of transition. Such a comment assumes that values have been lost, although it does not specify the nature of these values and, precisely because of its vagueness, it also fails to give any indication of what nature the values of the future may be. The root of this vagueness and the uneasiness that goes with it lie in the fact that we dream and mythicize—activities that reflect man's more or less perpetual feeling of discontent. But the dreaming of dreams and the building of myths are not separate parts of us; they are ourselves as whole individuals. To see them as parts quickly undermines the unity and wholeness of the individual, and he is soon 'in pieces' and does not know which way to go or even how to go. The moment a person loses his sense of wholeness and identity he also loses the sense of being related to his surroundings, be they persons or 'inanimate' nature. The disruption of the unity of the individual is not recognized to be present in the customary dichotomy of body and mind which, apart from the tedious literature about it with its aim of further fragmenting man, engenders more dreams and myths. When we were, and still are being, told that the 'objective' world of physical nature, to which our body that can be measured, weighed and dissected into 'parts and pieces' belongs, was and is radically different from the 'subjective' world of the 'mind', the tendency has been and still is to pursue the mechanical and measureable aspects of nature and to put one's confidence in techniques and gadgets which aid us in mastering and manipulating things: is man not just one of the things of nature, and is it not a fact that the chemistry of our body is of the same nature as that of organic matter? Still, this 'objective' evidence is constantly disturbed by 'subjective' intrusions which eventually, so it is hoped, will be 'objectified' and fitted into the mechanics of what is called 'life'. Certainly, it is easy to see that this trend towards excluding and denigrating the 'inner' world of the live person is both an oversimplification and falsification of the basic problem: how is man to come to terms with himself by fulfilling his capacity to be? Needless to say, 'to be' does not mean to do simply what pops into one's head, and to 'fulfill one's capacity to be' is not just morbid introspection; rather, to be and to fulfill one's capacity is to be able to respond directly to a total situation.

Just as it is wrong to say that man has nowadays lost those values which once served as a unifying center—the moralist's utopia that things in the past have been better, and all that is needed is to bring them back and force them on others—so also it is false to assume that man can find a center of values in the future—the revolutionary's utopia that things will be better and that all that is needed is to destroy the present. In actual life, value is what we experience as connected with and related to the reality of our being. It is here that real learning sets in. Real learning is a far cry from actions by rote or rule, because in real learning we keep our eyes open to new possibilities, while rote activities merely intensify the habit of closing one's eyes and continuing to sleep.

Learning never occurs in a vacuum. As everyone knows, a person is influenced in a multitude of ways which, to put it bluntly, may either make him or destroy him. On the personal level this involves and is reflected in the teacher-student relationship. However, relationship is an abstract term that should not make us oblivious to the concrete fact that it is the quality of the teacher as well as that of the student that counts, and that where quality is absent trouble is the inevitable result. We have only to refer to the chaotic situation of our educational system to realize the validity of the above statement. The prevailing chaos is the direct outcome of the 'dehumanized' mechanistic view of life evolved in the past: the teacher as a mechanical entity in a mechanistic system offers the student as a mechanical receptor a program that has no content whatsoever or approaches the ideal zero level in order to accommodate the largest audience which, although consisting of individuals, is treated as a statistic. Quality is confused with quantity and to speak of quality is almost the same as to use foul language and is rapidly becoming one of modern man's taboos. But inasmuch as man is not a mechanical gadget, a computerized entity, he resents being treated as a mere 'thing' or a 'number' and he tries to change the situation. This could only be effective if it is realized that values are existential, not arbitrary pronouncements, and that in the drama of human existence it is on the basis of the quality of the teacher and the quality of the student that the value and the quality of life emerge as a wider horizon of meaning, not as a predetermined entity that can be shelved and later on taken out at will. The tragedy of the present situation which few dare to point out openly, lies in the fact that many 'teachers' are no teachers (because as the product of a rigid no-content program they know as little as or even less than their students), that many 'students' are no students (because they believe that they already have all the answers and hence need no content-filled program), and that only too often a 'program' is but an external fad that has become merely an end in itself and has little to do with man's quest for being.

Although reference has been made to the present, it should be borne in mind that time is irrelevant. The basic problem is how can the teacher-student relationship be fruitful, and this leads us to the central purpose of this essay.

Inasmuch as man's growth can be furthered or retarded by factors that have a direct bearing on it the importance of a competent teacher is paramount. So also 'Jigs-med gling-pa (1729 or 30 to 1798) states:

> *So that the quality of all teaching reaches its perfection*
> *You should attach yourself to competent persons.*
> *In the same way as ordinary logs lying about*
> *In the forests and fields of the Malaya mountains*
> *Assume the fragrance of sandal from fresh branches,*
> *So also one follows in the steps of those on whom one relies.*[1]

Admittedly, it is not always easy to find a competent person, but there are indications that such persons exist. They are those who within their social status not only heed the obligations that go with it but also have learning and compassion:

> *Although a person in whom all qualities are perfectly present*
> *May be difficult to find in view of the power of restricting forces, you should depend on one whose mind is saturated with learning and compassion*
> *Within the framework of the pure foundation of what is permissible and what is not in the three levels of personality;*[2]
> *Who is well-versed in the ocean-wide rites of the Sutras and Tantras,*
> *Who is rich in the flawless fruit of a pristine awareness that comes from renunciation and realization,*
> *Who by the multicolored flower of four attractions*
> *Gathers around him worthy students like bees.*
> *In particular, the teacher*[3] *who imparts the instruction*
> *Is one who has received the initiatory empowerments, abides by his commitment and is very calm,*
> *Has imbibed the meaning of existence as it (proceeds) (from) the ground, (along) the path, (to) the goal,*
> *In whom the signs of realization through reverence are complete and whose being is free through understanding,*
> *Whose compassion is infinite and whose concern is solely for others,*
> *Who has little interest in ordinary affairs, but earnestly thinks about reality,*
> *Who is averse to (the ordinary way of*

life) and urges others (to follow his example),
Who is wise in the appropriate means (to guide) and in whom the wealth of realization through historical tradition is alive—[4]
If you depend on such a teacher, achievements will come quickly.[5]

This passage emphasizes what we are used to calling 'human qualities' and the implication is that a 'good' teacher teaches more by example than by words or the verbiage that is let loose on us in order to conceal the lack of qualities and of existential knowledge. Moreover, a 'good' teacher is not a busybody, meddling in all and everything—'being involved' in the jargon of contemporary hollow people. Rather he thinks seriously about the fact that life has meaning and is valuable because value is intrinsic to being (*chos*). Therefore he also has no need to cut himself off from tradition or to rebel against it (*byin-rlabs*).

On the other hand 'Jigs-med gling-pa has some harsh words to say about those who merely pretend and spend their time in superficialities concerned only with their own prestige, and thrive on the ignorance of those whom they are supposed to educate:[6]

Those teachers of the way that are like a wooden water-mill,
Watchful of their lineage like the Brahmins or
Afraid of losing their prestigious home, in ponds
Perform ablutions in which the result of learning and thinking has no place,
Or those friends that are like a frog in a pond,
In no way different from ordinary people
But raised to high positions by trusting fools
And puffed up by goods and honors showered on them,
Or those eccentric guides
Who have but little knowledge and go against their status and commitments,
Though lower than ordinary beings risen to the high heavens,
Cutting away the rope of love and compassion—
From them only evil spreads.
In particular, if one relies by virtue of his fame
On someone who has no superior qualities to one's own
And is without the bodhicitta,[7]
One (relies) on a blind leader, thoroughly mistaken,
And gropes around in the dense darkness (that are) false friends.
Therefore if one does not thoroughly investigate the teacher,
The merits of him who trusts (such a person) become exhausted
And having once obtained this human existence, he
Is tricked out of it like the one who mistook a poisonous snake for the shadow of a tree.

It is easy to recognize elements that are found in the contemporary scene: the claptrap of those catering for popularity, the scholastic preoccupation with pretentious trivialities and the hankering after ephemeral success, all of which is meant to take in the unwary. But while the fact cannot be denied that such features are widespread it does not follow that they are all that is, and more so, it does not follow that the unsatisfactory situation is without exception due to the teacher, although people with vested interest vociferously try to put the blame on the teacher and to exonerate the unworthy student. To the extent that there are incompetent 'teachers', there are 'students' who will not make the slightest effort, and to the same extent that there are competent teachers there are also worthy students. 'Jigs-med gling-pa is quite explicit on this matter:[8]

> There is no use of nectar when there is no vessel for it;
> Having become satisfied with mere trifles
> He shines with his fake trust like the changing seasons:
> First, not setting out on the path to reality he is like a wild ox,
> Then, being sick and tired of listening and thinking, he is engrossed in this life, and
> Lastly, siding with evil friends
> He oversteps the barriers of behavior and is like a savage from the jungle.

In his auto-commentary,[9] 'Jigs-med gling-pa, elaborating on this aphorism, well describes drifters and drop-outs:

An unworthy student, evil by upbringing and by nature, full of doubt and self-conceitedness, having thrown self-respect and decorum to the wind, resentful and highly emotional, jealous and nasty, not thinking about commitments and obligations, in no way a vessel that could hold the profound essence of reality consisting of such qualities as trust, discernment, diligence, and the certainty about freedom, will not see the qualities of a teacher. Himself not being calm he will see all his evil thoughts aroused by his emotional instability as the faults of the teacher, and while he may develop a little trust and awareness when he receives gifts and goods from the teacher's possession, wealth, and spiritual endowments, the trust is but artificial and as unstable as the change of the four seasons and the morning and afternoon warmth of the sun. When such a person is seriously advised to 'strive for happiness in this life here and in the hereafter', or 'to set out on the path of the Buddhist teaching', he fidgets about and tries to run away as if he had come close to an unmanageable mountain goat. Even if he has started on the path towards reality, he gets sick and tired of the very words 'learning', 'thinking', 'contemplating', and thinks as if to enter the gates of learning were intended only as a means of increasing the fickle achievements in his life. Lastly, should his mind tend a little towards learning, thinking and contemplating, he thinks that the acquisition of happiness and wealth in this triple world is the real meaning of life, or since nothing surpasses the status of the god Brahma or a universal ruler, this evil-minded person is made miserable by his fear that if one single person from this world of desires were to gain Buddhahood, his domain would be diminished, and as his mind is not working properly Māra's arrow enters his heart. As is stated in the Vajraśikhara (rdo rje rtse-mo):

> *Obstacles are not anywhere else:*
> *One's own mind is Māra.*

In the wake of such perversion he first, being afraid to voice his intentions in the presence of the teacher, deceives both the teacher and his co-students by pretending that the words 'by this spiritual progress will increase' or 'one should go into retreat' are his (real) thoughts. The moment he has left the monastery, his real intentions come to light. Then, since the world is full of fools and evil friends, he associates and makes friends with them, and it does not matter whether they are decent people or not. His mind is overpowered by desires, yearnings, and infatuations, like a savage from the jungle, and his way of behavior is like the tip of grass blown in all directions by the wind.

And he sums up this description by stating:[10]

> *While living close to a competent person they are quick to run away,*
> *Wherever they tend to go they are taken hold of by evil persons.*
> *While exhorted to live in solitude, what little moral decency they have, breaks down,*
> *They are like the tips of grass bending with the wind.*

As is obvious from this account, one of the characteristics of the unworthy student is his unwillingness to make any effort as it is so much easier to avoid any challenge, in particular the, challenge to mold himself and to struggle through to his real being. Certainly, it is easier to give in to any random impulse and to relax into the lowest common denominator of whims, inclinations, fads and escapades which only to often are nurtured by the feeling of resentment and the desire 'to get even' with somebody else—a low-level mentality whose hallmark is politics. The unwillingness to make any efforts is most marked in the attitude of getting easy answers to questions that have not been asked and 'to get away with' anything in order to turn it into easy cash. This person, well known to anyone who has to deal with students, is one who scrapes through the courses he has to attend within a program of his choice or one that has been suggested to him, then waits for his graduation and thereafter presents his degree certificate on the labor market. In a more picturesque language Klong-chen rab-'byams-pa (1308-1363) declares:

> *Those who do not care for their obligations and commitments and do nothing against their shortcomings,*

> *Thoroughly infatuated, of little intelligence, but difficult to satisfy,*
> *In whom anger and angry words increase and multiply,*
> *Attach themselves to a teacher with five wrong notions:*
> *The teacher is the deer, the teaching the musk,*
> *He himself the hunter, his efforts the arrow,*
> *And the result he gets is to be sold somewhere else.*
> *Being without principle they will suffer here and in the hereafter.*[11]

While the quality of the teacher is of paramount importance in the growth of the student and the selection of a teacher must be based on the fact that he himself has gone through the process of growth, that he has been willing to learn and continues learning from his own experience and not from the textbooks of a program, and that he knows how hard is the struggle to grow, it would be a mistake to assume that just because of his quality and qualification as a teacher any odd person can be sent to him. Not even the most gifted and competent teacher can do anything with a student who is unwilling and sees education as a confirmation of his preconceived immature notions. Hence the importance of finding out who is a worthy student. This does not imply discrimination against anyone, but is based on the observable fact of the difference between living individuals. Discrimination enters the picture when the attempt to grow is prevented by setting up 'norms' that are quantified nothingness. 'Jigs-med gling-pa significantly declares.[12]

> *It is important to investigate whether*
> *Someone devotes himself to finding himself in good faith*
> *Or craves for the goods of this seeming life*
> *Or is one so dull that he does not bother about the one or the other.*

He elaborates on this aphorism:[13]

> *There is no certainty as to the way in which one begins pursuing the path toward real being; some do so in good faith, some by covetousness, and others by just not bothering one way or another. Those who do so in good faith, know that teacher and teaching are related to each other, they are certain that they will realize freedom from worldliness, they delight in objects worthy of worship and the requisites for worship, they honor the Three Jewels and are generous in their gifts, motivated by trust they seriously listen, think and contemplate and immediately as well as subsequently benefit themselves and others. Those who do so by covetousness may sometimes attach themselves to a teacher and the teaching in their base motivations supported by passions and hatred for their pleasures, joys, and fame belonging to this life, and without giving any serious consideration to thoughts and contemplation that would set them free from Samsara with certainty, they take the empowerments and permissions and*

search for personal gains; their actions are not prompted by thoughts about the well-being of others, they harbor poisonous thoughts and intentions that are motivated by various activities or by arrogance and jealousy, they deck themselves up with objects and utensils not suited for the worship of the Three Jewels and the ritual of the Developing and Fulfillment Stages. They are the ones who want to fool themselves and others. Those who do not bother one way or another are the dull fools who avoid the previous two possibilities; without having faith in or a desire for real being, they imitate and mimic others and what others do, like a monkey sitting in meditation or a parrot intoning spells, and in the end, not observing any commitments or obligations, they are like stray dogs roaming about in alleys. Therefore the first type, since he is a willing person, has to be accepted; the two others may be shown kindness as pupils at a later stage by setting them on the true path by many appropriate means and prognoses and by special ways of expressing the good wishes for them.

No doubt, these are harsh words and yet there is a deep feeling of compassion for the unfortunate who do not have the sense of seeing that life is meaningful in itself, that its meaning is never an outward tag, and that man has to bring it out in himself by using his potentialities. The acknowledgement of the differences in individuals makes it possible to 'educate' them, which can never be equated with 'fitting a person into a pattern', with insisting on conformity and in hunting down the person who does not conform to the 'pattern' as seems to be the accepted form in our Western society. The Buddhist would simply say: "Look, I cannot accept you as a disciple now, you still have a long way to go, but when you have learned from your mistakes and are serious about growing up, I shall readily accept you and guide you."

There are, of course, always only a few who would qualify as worthy students whom Klong-chen rab-'byams-pa characterizes as follows:[14]

> *The worthy students, trustful and highly discerning,*
> *Diligent, conscientious, circumspect and knowledgeable,*
> *Not going beyond (the teacher's) word, observing their obligations and commitments,*
> *Controlled in body, speech and mind, compassionate and deeply concerned about others' well-being,*
> *Accommodating, patient, generous, and visionary,*
> *Steady and deeply devoted, will*
> *Always be mindful of the teacher's qualities.*
> *They will not look for faults and even if they see them will consider them as qualities.*
> *By thinking from the bottom of their hearts that they are certainly their own*

>   (mistaken) views and not existing in
>   (the teacher)
>   And use admission (of their shortcomings) and self-restraint as counteragents (to their error).

The first section of this passage may be said simply to point out and to list those qualities in a student which every teacher would like to see in the person whom he is going to teach. When 'Jigs-med gling-pa sums them up in the words:[15]

>   Trusting, discerning, willing to listen,
>   deeply compassionate,
>   Delighting in fulfilling one's obligations
>   and commitments, controlled in body,
>   speech and mind,
>   Accommodating, generous, visionary,
>   and conscientious,

and then explains them in terms of a gradation:

>   While in previous ages there were many noble teachers and saints as well as amazingly worthy students and many vessels were richly filled with qualities by trust alone, the teacher's spirituality and understanding and the students' unlimited devotion and reverence combined, just as when the milk flows automatically into the mouth of the calf if it is near its mother cow, in this evil age such conditions are difficult to bring about by assembling them from many regions. If in addition to trust on the student's part there is no discernment, the essence of reality will not be understood; if there is no willingness to listen, good and evil will not be recognized; if there is no compassion, there will be a relapse in the level of a Śrāvaka or Pratyekabuddha in spite of the fact that one is interested in the Mahāyāna; if one does not bother about obligations and commitments, one mistakes medicine for poison; if one is not calm in body, speech and mind, the rain of moral violations falls; if one is not accommodating, one cannot get along with one's friends and relatives; if one is not generous, the accumulation of one's merits collapses; if one has no visions, the world of appearance comes as an enemy; if one is not conscientious and has no self-respect, one cannot learn the way of the noble. Therefore when one is constantly aware of the fact that the faults are with us alone and, not paying any attention to the faults of others, follows the path toward real being by relying on friends concerned with one's well-being, one possesses a great wealth. By thinking that it is I who am lacking in this or that particular quality of a disciple, one has begun to struggle against one's own shortcomings,

he may have fallen a prey to the myth that things were better in the past, but at the same time he underscores Klong-chen rab-'byams-pa's profound psychological insight. Technically this is known as projection, which is a process by which we attribute traits within ourselves to others and assume them to have an independent existence. To admit that projection takes place is already a step in the direction of accepting oneself and of attempting to restore one's integrity. Insofar as we see ourselves in and through the other there arises within us the conflict of contrary emotions; we either become inordinately attached to or shrink in aversion from what we see and, in the latter case, we even tend to re-inforce our ego defenses which always have inhibited the acceptance of ourselves, by a further projection: "I do not do such a thing, but others do lots of such things," and often this projection comes as a means to conceal the wish "If only I could do such a thing!" The conflict of the emotions is like a disease, we may struggle *against* it which only means to force sickness into a new channel—we may relieve a headache by some drug or other only to upset the stomach and have another problem on hand. Or we may accept the disease as an opportunity for re-orientation and for rebuilding ourselves. Both Klong-chen rab-'byams-pa and 'Jigs-med gling-pa, using a famous passage from an early Sūtra, the Gaṇḍavyūhasūtra, illustrate what happens or should happen in a proper teacher-student relationship, by reference to a patient:

> *Just as a patient is in need of a physician,*
> *People of a ruler, a lonely traveller of an escort,*
> *A merchant of a leader, a boatman of a boat,*
> *So in order to quiet the emotions, to make evil harmless,*
> *To overcome birth and death, to have the two aspects of reality being spontaneously present,*
> *To cross the ocean of worldiness, you must rely on a teacher.*
> *Do so by four positive ideas,*
> *As in so doing all other methods are outweighed:*
> *The teacher is the physician, his instruction the medicine,*
> *You yourself the patient,*
> *And your effort is the application of the medicine,*

says Klong-chen rab-'byams-pa,[16] while 'Jigs-med gling-pa states:[17]

> *Rely on a teacher in fear of the enemy who is birth and death and the emotions,*
> *As a sick person will depend on a physician, a lonely traveller on an escort,*
> *A timid person on what the seasons forebode, and a merchant on a leader,*
> *And a boatman on his boat.*

Obviously, the analogy of sickness is extremely significant. Health cannot be simply defined as the absence of sickness, rather it is the other way round; health is the basic state of a live person and sickness a disturbance in this state, and only the ability to recognize and accept sickness will determine the capacity to experience health, or in other words, the capacity to experience health is tied to the ability to recognize and feel the painfulness of a state of sickness. This recognition implies or leads to a willingness to do something about this unpleasant situation; this willingness must come from the patient—in our case, the student. Here he is in dire need of help which can only come from a physician, in this case the teacher, who is looking for health and not content or complacent with handing the patient-student a prescription drug or program that under favorable conditions will only fit the person into the 'sick' society. Thus the teacher, the student, and the content of the teaching are all inextricably interconnected with each other in a situation that is ever new.

1. The Collected Works of Kun-mkhyen 'Jigs-med gling-pa vol. I, p. 250.
2. The three levels are explained as referring to (a) a person who belongs to any group mentioned in the Prātimokṣa (discipline to be followed by these persons as detailed, for instance, in Abhidharmakośa IV, 14ff.), (b) a Bodhisattva whose obligations and duties far exceed those of the members of the previous group, and (c) a *rig-'dzin*, i.e. a person who has an immediate grasp of a situation and spontaneosuly can respond to it.
3. The text uses here the word *bla-ma* by which always someone who has realized what it means to be, is meant, and very often this term marks the transition from the without to the within.
4. *brgyud-pa'i byin-rlabs-dan*: In the flux of human history we find personalities who can arouse us to find for ourselves what it means to be. By leading us to reflect upon our being they themselves are within the tradition (*brgyud*) and as examples sustain our own efforts (*byin-rlabs*).
5. The collected works of Kun-mkhyen 'Jigs-med gling-pa, vol. I, pp. 251-254.
6. ibid., pp. 255-258.
7. *bodhicitta*: The Tibetan interpretation of this term is that it is the dynamic life force that urges us on to rediscover our being. It is not a 'thought' but that which makes thinking possible.
8. The Collected Works of Kun-mkhyen 'Jigs-med gling-pa, vol. I, p. 264.
9. ibid., pp. 264ff.
10. ibid., p. 265.
11. rDzogs-pa-chen-po Sems-nyid ngal-gso, fol. 21b.
12. The Collected Works of Kun-mkhyen 'Jigs-med gling-pa, vol. I, p. 268.
13. ibid., p. 268f.
14. rDzogs-pa chen-po Sems-nyid ngal-gso, fol. 229.
15. The Collected Works of Kun-mkhyen 'Jigs-med gling-pa, vol. I, p. 271.
16. rDzogs-pa-chen-po Sems-nyid ngal-gso, fol. 21b.
17. The Collected Works of Kun-mkhyen 'Jigs-med gling-pa, vol. I, p. 262.

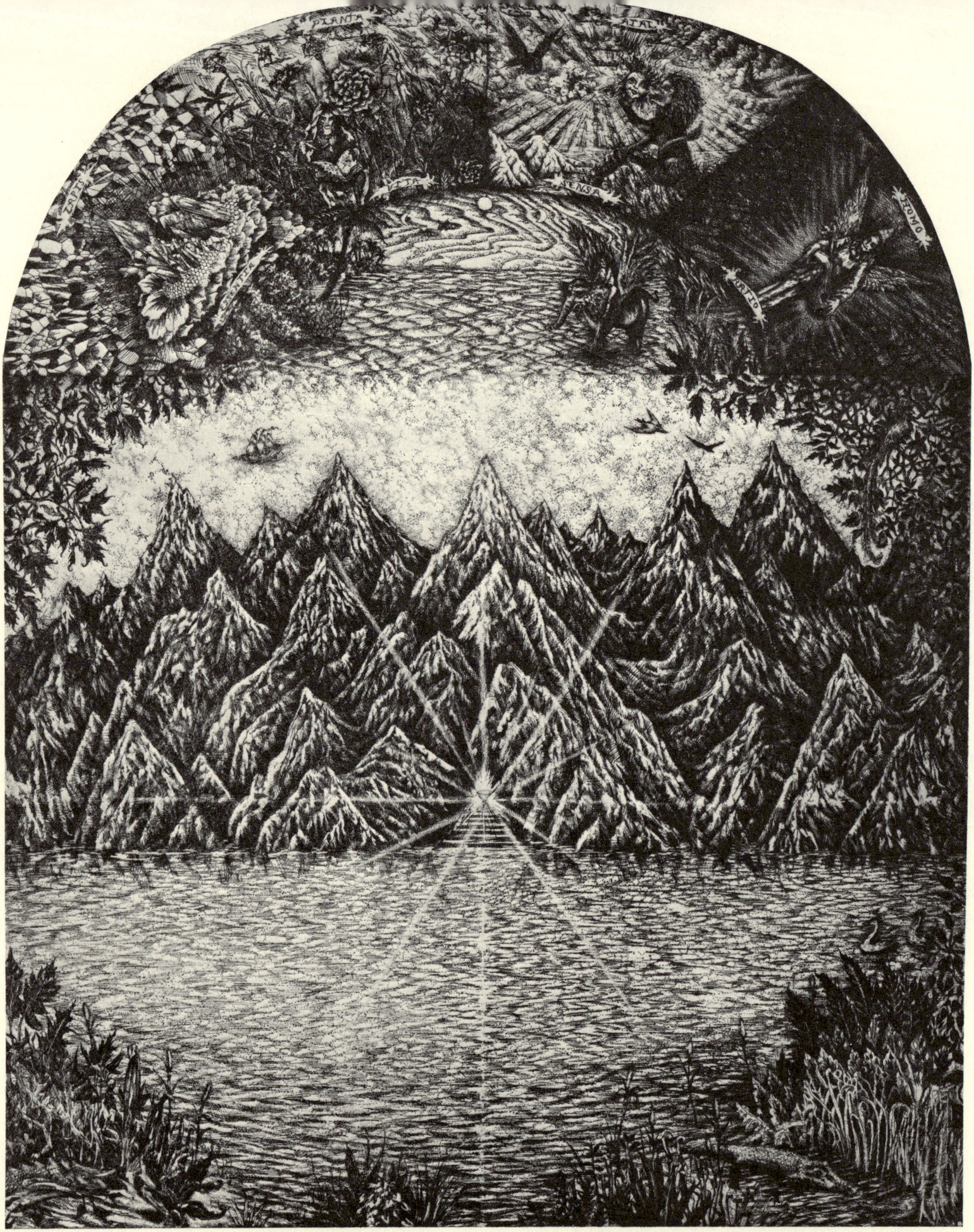

Memorables

René Daumal

Remember: your mother and your father, and your first lie, the indiscrete odor of which crawls in your memory.

Remember your first insult to those who made you: the seed of pride was sown, the crack glistened, breaking the night one.

Remember the evenings of terror when the thought of the void scratched your stomach, and always returned like a vulture, to nibble you; and remember the morning of sun in the room.

Remember the night of deliverance, when, your untied body falling like a veil, you breathed a little from the incorruptible air; and remember the clammy animals that took you back again.

Remember magics, fish and tenacious dreams;—you wanted to see, you stopped up your two eyes in order to see, without knowing how to open the other.

Remember your accomplices and your deceits, and that great desire to leave the cage.

Remember the day when you split open the web and were taken alive, fixed in place, in the uproar of uproars the wheel of wheels turning without turning, you inside, always snatched up by the same immobile moment, repeated, repeated, and time was making one turn only, everything turned in three innumerable directions, the time curled up backwards,—and the eyes of flesh saw only a dream, there only existed the devouring silence, words were dried skins and the noise, the yes, the noise, the no, the visible howl and darkness of the machine denied you,—the silent cry, 'I am' that the bone hears, from which the stone dies, from which that which never was believes to die,—and you were reborn in each instant only to be denied by the great circle without boundaries, all pure all center, pure except you.

And remember the days that followed, when you walked like a bewitched corpse, with the certainty of being eaten by the infinite, of being annulled by the only existing Absurd.

51

And above all, remember the day when you wanted to throw
out everything, no matter how,—but a guardian kept watch in
your night, he kept watch while you dreamed, he made you touch
your flesh, he made you remember your own, he made you gather
your rags,—remember your guardian.

Remember the beautiful mirage of concepts, and moving words,
palaces of mirrors built in a cave; and remember the man who came,
who broke everything, who took you with his rough hand, pulled you
from your dreams, and made you sit in the thorns of the full day;
and remember that you do not know how to remember yourself.

Remember that you have to pay for everything, remember your
happiness but when your heart was run over, it was too late to
pay in advance.

Remember the friend who spread out his reason to gather
your tears, spurting from the frozen source, violating the sun
of spring.

Remember that love triumphed when she and you knew how to
submit to its jealous fire, praying to die in the same flame.

But remember that love is of no one, that in your heart of
flesh is no one, that the sun is of no one, blush seeing the
swamp of your heart.

Remember the mornings when grace was like a raised club,
that led you, submissive through your days,—happy the cattle
beneath the yoke.

And remember that your poor memory let the golden fish flow
between its numbed fingers.

Remember those who say to you: Remember,—remember the
voice that said to you: don't fall,—and remember the dubious
pleasure of the fall.

Remember, poor memory, mine, the two faces of the medallion
and its unique metal.

Translated by Louise Landes-Levi

Being Related

Graham Parkes

*Why is there anything at all,
and not rather nothing?*

To many people this question may at first seem a typical example of abstract, "ivory tower" philosophy. I hope to show that, on the contrary, it is the most concrete and vitally "relevant" question a person can ask, and one that *every* individual has to try to answer—or at least to take a stand on—at some point in his or her life. In questioning the individual's relation to Being, we question the meaning of our existence. It is thus the question "Who am I?"

The authentic posing of this question is by no means a detached philosophical enterprise: it is rather to allow the question to take over one's whole being and shake it to the foundations. For some people the question first arises in childhood (when it can be quite a terrifying experience, the first intimation of one's extreme mortality) and continues to break into their existence with varying intensity throughout the course of their lives. Others would deny that such a "metaphysical" question had any meaning for them, with the implication that one would do far better to get on with the business of living than worry about such abstract and ethereal concerns. However, the question is one that touches *everybody's* being at some time in their life, even if the most frequent response to it is an abrupt turning away from it in favor of the concerns of "the real world."

How does it feel to ask this question in an authentic way? It is important to see first of all that the question is different from any "why" question we might ask concerning events *within* the world, since it is not asking for a cause or a reason, but rather a ground. What is here being put in question is not just any particular thing, nor even the totality of presently existing things, but also whatever has been and will be and could possibly be—in short, everything that is not simply nothing. In most instances it is truer to say not that the totality of what is is *put* into question, but rather that it *comes* into question of its own accord. The question usually announces itself to us when we are gripped by intense moods, such as extreme despair, or boundless ecstasy, or—most commonly—an all-pervading "cosmic" boredom. It is as if we are seeing the world for the first time: the totality of existing things seems to *be* in a completely new and different way. The experience can be accompanied by a spectrum of affects ranging from joyful wonder and awe at the *thatness* of things—that things simply *are*—through the feeling that they are what they are not "in themselves" but in as far as I *let them be*, to acute anxiety at the realization that everything might just as well *not be*, that I am correspondingly constantly the possibility of *not* being, that I might cease to be at any moment.

Historically Western metaphysics and theology have sought the ground of all that is in terms of an ultimate cause or reason, and their questing has ended with the unmoved mover, or with God, or with Being. In this century Martin Heidegger, one of the most profound thinkers ever, has attempted to re-awaken in us a sense of the necessity of asking the question of (our relation to) Being —and in a way that prepares us for the possibility of realizing that the ground (*Grund*) of all that is, Being, is also an abyss (*Abgrund*) of no-thingness, or non-Being. This no-thingness (akin to the notion of *shunyata* in Mahayana Buddhism), is not a sterile void, but is rather a realm of absolute freedom pregnant with possibility. Why is there anything rather than nothing? There is no pre-existent reason in and of itself: there is only the meaning each individual creates for him or herself.

As humans we are distinguished from other beings by the fact that we are able, by relating to our death as the constant possibility of non-Being, to relate to Being. Being, not itself a *being* (or entity) but the absolutely *other* to all that is, cannot be described but only named (poetically) or symbolized. But in so far as it can be named it can be *thought*— and it is a certain kind of *thinking* which constitutes the human being's relation to Being, and which thus provides us with the possibility of grappling with the question of Being.

Let us consider this kind of thinking, which Heidegger sometimes calls "meditative thinking." (The German word for "meditative" also has the connotations of *meaning* in the deepest sense, and of *sensing*; so that it is as much a *feeling* as a thinking. It is interesting to bear in mind that our word "meditate" comes from a Latin verb meaning "to attend to medically, with an aim towards curing.") Meditative thinking is neither theoretical nor conceptual, but merely contemplative; it is rather a *doing*, but a doing that requires all the care and attention of the sculptor at the block or the potter at the wheel. It is not concerned with the "transcendental," with something "above and beyond" the phenomenal world, but rather with that which lies closest to us, and which we thus constantly overlook. Being simple, thinking is—for most of us—very difficult; but it is something of which *every* human being is capable, since we are by nature the being who can thinkingly relate to Being.

The preparation for thinking consists in a *non-willing*. We must willingly (and so somewhat paradoxically) give up the exercise of the will, and so attain an attitude towards the world which Heidegger calls *Gelassenheit*. *Gelassenheit*—an almost impossible word to translate—is a key term in the work of Eckhart and Boehme, where it means the attitude of renouncing the individual will in order to enter into harmony with the will of God. In Heidegger the word has lost its theological overtones, and means simply a relaxed *letting-be*. Not a letting-be in the sense of a totally passive letting every thing run its own course, nor yet a letting that imposes one's will on the world (as in "Let thy will be done"). Like the Taoist notion of *wu wei* (action in inaction), and also like the "non-doing" of Castaneda's Don Juan, *Gelassenheit* is an attitude that lies outside the realm of activity and passivity. *"There will be an answer, let it be."*

Just as we cannot *try* to be relaxed, so we cannot will ourselves to be *gelassen*; and indeed *Gelassenheit* also has the connotation of being *let in* from without, let into us by Being itself. Therefore the essence of *Gelassenheit* is an awake *waiting*, but a waiting in which we *leave open* what it is we are waiting for. The idea is to open ourselves up completely, emptying ourselves of all preconceptions and expectations of what is going to happen, and to *attend* (the root meaning of which is "stretch towards") carefully to what is going on. If we attend patiently, we will find developing a new sense of rootedness in the earth and relatedness to our ground. We will realize that everything *is* only in relation to its opposite, and by accepting that any revealing is always balanced by a concealment, we will find ourselves at that still point where we can embrace the opposites through opening ourselves to the mystery of Being. We will experience a loosening of the restrictions of the distinction between subject and object: things will no longer appear as *objects,* i.e. as stable, enduring entities which we represent to ourselves as standing over against us, but they will rather, to use Heidegger's words, "rest in the dynamic return to the abiding of the expanse of their self-belonging." Such poetical language (it comes across much better in the German!) is necessary because our everyday language, impregnated as it is with several centuries of seeing human beings as subjects in a world of objects, is inadequate to the task of describing experiences which undercut the subject-object dichotomy. It may be easier to relate to Heidegger's descriptions in the light of the experience of artistic and creative inspiration, mystical or psychedelic experience, or the practice of prayer and meditation in certain religions. As with all true meditation, the thinking of Being does not aim at *results*: we think Being because to do so is to express our deepest nature.

To talk about our *relation* to Being is somewhat misleading, if it suggests that Being is an entity with which we, as entities ourselves, can come into a relation. Moving into the realm of the figurative in an attempt to characterize the relation, we might say that Being appropriates human beings to itself by *sending* or *giving* itself in calling to them. The appropriate way to *thank* Being for giving itself to us is to *think* it; and what we realize when we think Being in the right way is that we *belong* to Being. By waiting and attentively listening for the voice of Being, we can cut short our longing by realizing our *be-longing*, by realizing that we have been in tune with Being all along. To say that we be-long to Being is not just to say that we are a part of the cosmic whole. If we look on ourselves merely as beings among others, then it is true to say that as such we belong to the totality of the universe. But we can also consider ourselves as pure Being-there (*Da-sein*), as partaking in that pure open-ness which lets all beings be what they are—and in this sense as belonging to Being.

    Our relation to Being is a strange one, since Being is itself the mysterious. It shows itself to us only in the mode of withdrawing from us; it is closer to us than any particular being, but at the same time it is the farthest away. The root meaning of the word "relation" is "carrying back." In relating to Being we must let ourselves into its nearness and so carry ourselves back to our original home.

L'Habitude
Sully Prudhomme

L'habitude est une étrangère
Qui supplante en nous la raison.
C'est une ancienne ménagère
Qui s'installe dans la maison.

Elle est discrète, humble, fidèle,
Familière avec tous les coins;
On ne s'occupe jamais d'elle,
Car elle a d'invisibles soins:

Elle conduit les pieds de l'homme,
Sait le chemin qu'il eût choisi,
Connaît son but sans qu'il le nomme,
Et lui dit tout bas: 'Par ici'.

Travaillant pour nous en silence,
D'un gest sûr, toujours pareil,
Elle a l'oeil de la vigilance,
Les lèvres douctes du sommeil.

Habit is an outsider
Who supplants the intellect in us.
She is an old housekeeper
Who makes herself at home.

She is discreet, humble, faithful,
Familiar with all the corners;
She never attracts attention,
For her tasks are invisible:

She guides a man's feet,
Knows the road that he might have chosen,
Knows his goals without his naming it,
And says to him, Softly: "This way".

Working for us in silence,
With a steady hand, always the same,
She has a watchful eye,
Lips sweet with sleep.

translated by Karl Ray

When Speaking on Different Subjects

A Talk by G. I. Gurdjieff

When speaking on different subjects, I have noticed how difficult it is to pass on one's understanding, even of the most ordinary subject and to a person well known to me. Our language is too poor for full and exact descriptions. Later I found that this lack of understanding between one man and another is a mathematically ordered phenomenon as precise as the multiplication table. It depends in general on the so-called "psyche" of the people concerned, and in particular on the state of their psyche at any given moment.

The truth of this law can be verified at every step. In order to be understood by another man, it is not only necessary for the speaker to know how to speak but for the listener to know how to listen. This is why I can say that if I were to speak in a way I consider exact, everybody here, with very few exceptions, would think I was crazy. But since at present I have to speak to my audience as it is, and my audience will have to listen to me, we must first establish the possibility of a common understanding.

In the course of our talk we must gradually mark the signposts of a productive conversation. All I wish to suggest now is that you try to look at things and phenomena around you, and especially at yourselves, from a point of view, from an angle, that may be different from what is usual or natural to you. Only to look, for to do more is possible only with the wish and cooperation of the listener, when the listener ceases to listen passively and begins to do, that is, when he moves into an active state.

Very often in conversation with people, one hears the direct or implied view that man as we meet with him in ordinary life could be regarded as almost the center of the universe, the "crown of creation," or at any rate that he is a large and important entity; that his possibilities are almost unlimited, his powers almost infinite. But even with such views there are a number of reservations: they say that, for this, exceptional conditions are necessary, special circumstances, inspiration, revelation and so on.

However, if we examine this conception of "man," we see at once that it is made up of features which belong not to one man but to a number of known or supposed separate individuals. We never meet such a man in real life, neither in the present nor as a historical personage in the past. For every man has his own weaknesses and if you look closely the mirage of greatness and power disintegrates.

But the most interesting thing is not that people clothe others in this mirage but that, owing to a peculiar feature of their own psyche, they transfer it to themselves, if not in its entirety, at least in part as a reflection. And so, although they are almost nonentities, they imagine themselves to be that collective type or not far removed from it.

But if a man knows how to be sincere with himself—not sincere as the word is usually understood, but mercilessly sincere—then, to the question "What are you?" he will not expect a comforting reply. So now, without waiting for you to come nearer to experiencing for yourselves what I am speaking about, I suggest that, in order to understand better what I mean, each of you should now ask himself the question "What am I?" I am certain that 95 percent of you will be puzzled by this question and will answer with another one: "What do you mean?"

And this will prove that a man has lived all his life without asking himself this question, has taken for granted, as axiomatic, that he is "something," even something very valuable, something he has never questioned. At the same time he is unable to explain to another what this something is, unable to convey even any idea of it, for he himself does not know what it is. Is the reason he does not know, because, in fact, this "something" does not exist but is merely assumed to exist? Is it not strange that people pay so little attention to themselves in the sense of self-knowledge? Is it not strange with what dull complacency they shut their eyes to what they really are and spend their lives in the pleasant conviction that they represent something valuable? They fail to see the galling emptiness hidden behind the highly painted facade created by their self-delusion and do not realize that its value is purely conventional.

True, this is not always so. Not everyone looks at himself so superficially. There do exist enquiring minds, which long for the truth of the heart, seek it, strive to solve the problems set by life, try to penetrate to the essence of things and phenomena and to penetrate into themselves. If a man reasons and thinks soundly, no matter what path he follows in solving these problems, he must inevitably arrive back at himself, and begin with the solution of the problem of what he is himself and what his place is in the world around him. For without this knowledge, he will have no focal point in his search. Socrates' words "Know thyself" remain for all those who seek true knowledge and being.

I have just used a new word—"being." To make sure that we all understand the same thing by it, I shall have to say a few words in explanation.

We have just been questioning whether what a man thinks about himself corresponds to what he is in reality, and you have asked yourselves what you are. Here is a doctor, there an engineer, there an artist. Are they in reality what we think they are? Can we treat the personality of each one as identical with his profession, with the experience which that profession, or the preparation for it, has given him?

Every man comes into the world like a clean sheet of paper; and then the people and circumstances around him begin vying with each other to dirty this sheet and to cover it with writing. Education, the formation of morals, information we call knowledge—all feelings of duty, honor, conscience and so on—enter here. And they all claim that the methods adopted for grafting these shoots known as man's "personality" to the trunk are immutable and infallible. Gradually the sheet is dirtied, and the dirtier with so-called "knowledge" the sheet becomes, the cleverer the man is considered to be. The more writing there is in the place called "duty," the more honest the possessor is said to be; and so it is with everything. And the dirty sheet itself, seeing that people consider its "dirt" as merit, considers it valuable. This is an example of what we call "man," to which we often even add such words as talent and genius. Yet our "genius" will have his mood spoiled for the whole day if he does not find his slippers beside his bed when he wakes up in the morning.

A man is not free either in his manifestations or in his life. He cannot be what he wishes to be and what he thinks he is. He is not like his picture of himself, and the words "man, the crown of creation" do not apply to him.

"Man"—this is a proud term, but we must ask ourselves what kind of man? Not the man, surely, who is irritated at trifles, who gives his attention to petty matters and gets involved in everything around him. To have the right to call himself a man, he must be a man; and this "being" comes only through self-knowledge and work on oneself in the directions that become clear through self-knowledge.

Have you ever tried to watch yourself mentally when your attention has not been set on some definite problem for concentration? I suppose most of you are familiar with this, although perhaps only a few have systematically watched it in themselves. You are no doubt aware of the way we think by chance association, when our thought strings disconnected scenes and memories together, when everything that falls within the field of our consciousness, or merely touches it lightly, calls up these chance associations in our thought. The string of thoughts seems to go on uninterruptedly, weaving together fragments of representations of former perceptions, taken from different recordings in our memories. And these recordings turn and unwind while our thinking apparatus deftly weaves its threads of thought continuously from this material. The records of our feelings revolve in the same way—pleasant and unpleasant, joy and sorrow, laughter and irritation, pleasure and pain, sympathy and antipathy. You hear yourself praised and you are pleased; someone reproves you and your mood is spoiled. Something new captures your interest and instantly makes you forget what interested you just as much the moment before. Gradually your interest attaches you to the new thing to such an extent that you sink into it from head to foot; suddenly you do not possess it any more, you have disappeared, you are bound to and dissolved in this thing; in fact it possesses you, it has captivated you, and this infatuation, this capacity for being captivated is, under many different guises, a property of each one of us. This binds us and prevents our being free. By the same token it takes away our strength and our time, leaving us no possibility of being objective and free—two essential qualities for anyone who decides to follow the way of self-knowledge.

We must strive for freedom if we strive for self-knowledge. The task of self-knowledge and of further self-development is of such importance and seriousness, it demands such intensity of effort, that to attempt it any old way and amongst other things is impossible. The person who undertakes this task must put it first in his life, which is not so long that he can afford to squander it on trifles.

What can allow a man to spend his time profitably in his search, if not freedom from every kind of attachment?

Freedom and seriousness. Not the kind of seriousness which looks out from under knitted brows with pursed lips, carefully restrained gestures and words filtered through the teeth, but the kind of seriousness that means determination and persistence in the search, intensity and constancy in it, so that a man, even when resting, continues with his main task.

Ask yourselves—are you free? Many are inclined to answer "yes," if they are relatively secure in a material sense and do not have to worry about the morrow, if they depend on no one for their livelihood or in the choice of their conditions of life. But is this freedom? Is it only a question of external conditions?

You have plenty of money, let us say. You live in luxury and enjoy general respect and esteem. The people who run your well-organized business are absolutely honest and devoted to you. In a word, you have a very good life. Perhaps you think so yourself and consider yourself wholly free, for after all your time is your own. You are a patron of the arts, you settle world problems over a cup of coffee and you may even be interested in the development of hidden spiritual powers. Problems of the spirit are not foreign to you and you are at home among philosophical ideas. You are educated and well read. Having some erudition in many fields, you are known as a clever man, for you find your way easily in all sorts of pursuits; you are an example of a cultured man. In short, you are to be envied.

In the morning you wake up under the influence of an unpleasant dream. The slightly depressed mood disappeared but has left its trace in a kind of lassitude and uncertainty of movement. You go to the mirror to brush your hair and by accident drop your hairbrush. You pick it up and just as you have dusted it off, you drop it again. This time you pick it up with a shade of impatience and because of that you drop it a third time. You try to grab it in midair but instead, it flies at the mirror. In vain you jump to catch it. Smash! . . . a star-shaped cluster of cracks appears in the antique mirror you were so proud of. Hell! The records of discontent begin to turn. You need to vent your annoyance on someone. Finding that your servant has forgotten to put the newspaper beside your morning coffee, your cup of patience overflows and you decide you can no longer stand the wretched man in the house.

Now it is time for you to go out. Taking advantage of the fine day, your destination not being far away, you decide to walk while your car follows slowly behind. The bright sun somewhat mollifies you. Your attention is attracted to a crowd that has gathered around a man lying unconscious on the pavement. With the help of onlookers the porter puts him into a cab and he is driven off to the hospital. Notice how the strangely familiar face of the driver is connected in your associations and reminds you of the accident you had last year. You were returning home from a gay birthday party. What a delicious cake they had there! This servant of yours who forgot your morning paper ruined your breakfast. Why not make up for it now? After all, cake and coffee are extremely important! Here is the fashionable café you sometimes go to with your friends. But why have you remembered about the accident? You had surely almost forgotten about the morning's unpleasantness. . . . And now, do your cake and coffee really taste so good?

You see the two ladies at the next table. What a charming blonde! She glances at you and whispers to her companion, "That's the sort of man I like."

Surely none of your troubles are worth wasting time on or getting upset about. Need one point out how your mood changed from the moment you met the blonde and how it lasted while you were with her? You return home humming a gay tune and even the broken mirror only provokes a smile. But what about the business you went out for in the morning? You have only just remembered it . . . that's clever! Still, it does not matter. You can telephone. You lift the receiver and the operator gives you the wrong number. You ring again and get the same number. Some man says sharply that he is sick of you—you say it is not your fault, an altercation follows and you are surprised to learn that you are a fool and an idiot, and if you call again . . . The rumpled carpet under your foot irritates you, and you should hear the tone of voice in which you reprove the servant who is handing you a letter. The letter is from a man you respect and whose good opinion you value. The contents of the letter are so flattering to you that your irritation gradually dies down and is replaced by the pleasantly embarrassed feeling that flattery arouses. You finish reading it in a most amiable mood.

I could continue this picture of your day

—you a free man. Perhaps you think I have been exaggerating. No, this is a true scenario taken from life.

This was a day in the life of a man well known both at home and abroad, a day reconstructed and described by him that same evening as a vivid example of associative thinking and feeling. Tell me where is the freedom when people and things possess a man to such an extent that he forgets his mood, his business and himself? In a man who is subject to such variation can there be any serious attitude toward his search?

You understand better now that a man need not necessarily be what he appears to be, that the question is not one of external circumstances and facts but of the inner structure of a man and of his attitude toward these facts. But perhaps this is only true for his associations; with regard to things he "knows" about, perhaps the situation is different.

But I ask you, if for some reason each of you was unable to put your knowledge to practical use for several years, how much would remain? Would this not be like having materials which in time dry up and evaporate? Remember the comparison with a clean sheet of paper. And indeed in the course of our life we are learning something the whole time, and we call the results of this learning "knowledge." And in spite of this knowledge, do we not often prove to be ignorant, remote from real life and therefore ill-adapted to it? We are half-educated like tadpoles, or more often simply "educated" people with a little information about many things but all of it is woolly and inadequate. Indeed it is merely information. We cannot call it knowledge, since knowledge is an inalienable property of a man; it cannot be more and it cannot be less. For a man "knows" only when he himself "is" that knowledge. As for your convictions—have you never known them to change? Are they not also subject to fluctuation like everything else in us? Would it not be more accurate to call them opinions rather than convictions, dependent as much on our mood as on our information or perhaps simply on the state of our digestion at a given moment?

Every one of you is a rather uninteresting example of an animated automaton. You think that a "soul," and even a "spirit," is necessary to do what you do and live as you live. But perhaps it is enough to have a key for winding up the spring of your mechanism. Your daily portions of food help to wind you up and renew the purposeless antics of associations again and again. From this background separate thoughts are selected and you attempt to connect them into a whole and pass them off as valuable and as your own. We also pick out feelings and sensations, moods and experiences and out of all this we create the mirage of an inner life, call ourselves conscious and reasoning beings, talk about God, about eternity, about eternal life and other higher matters; we speak about everything imaginable, judge and discuss, define and evaluate, but we omit to speak about ourselves and about our own real objective value, for we are all convinced that if there is anything lacking in us, we can acquire it.

If in what I have said I have succeeded even to a small extent in making clear in what chaos is the being we call man, you will be able to answer for yourselves the question of what he lacks and what he can obtain if he remains as he is, what of value he can add to the value he himself represents.

I have already said that there are people who hunger and thirst for truth. If they examine the problems of life and are sincere with themselves, they soon become convinced that it is not possible to live as they have lived and to be what they have been until now; that a way out of this situation is essential and that a man can develop his hidden capacities and powers only by cleaning his machine of the dirt that has clogged it in the course of his life. But in order to undertake this cleaning in a rational way, he has to see what needs to be cleaned, where and how; but to see this for himself is almost impossible. In order to see anything of this one has to look from the outside; and for this mutual help is necessary.

If you remember the example I gave of identification, you will see how blind a man is when he identifies with his moods, feelings and thoughts. But is our dependence on things only limited to what can be observed at first glance? These things are so much in relief that they cannot help catching the eye. You remember how we spoke about people's characters, roughly dividing them into good and bad? As a man gets to know himself, he continually finds new areas of his mechanicalness —let us call it automatism—domains where his will, his "I wish," has no power, areas not subject to him, so confused and subtle that it is impossible to find his way about in them without the help and the authoritative guidance of someone who knows.

This briefly is the state of things in the realm of self-knowledge: in order to do you must know; but to know you must find out how to know. We cannot find this out by ourselves.

Besides self-knowledge, there is another aspect of the search—self-development. Let us see how things stand there. It is clear that a man left to his own devices cannot wring out of his little finger the knowledge of how to develop and, still less, exactly what to develop in himself.

Gradually, by meeting people who are searching, by talking to them and by reading relevant books, a man becomes drawn into the sphere of questions concerning self-development.

But what may he meet here? First of all an abyss of the most unpardonable charlatanism, based entirely on the greed for making money by hoaxing gullible people who are seeking a way out of their spiritual impotence. But before a man learns to divide the wheat from the tares, a long time must elapse and perhaps the urge itself to find the truth will flicker and go out in him, or will become morbidly perverted and his blunted flair may lead him into such a labyrinth that the path out of it, figuratively speaking, will lead straight to the devil. If a man succeeds in getting out of this first swamp, he may fall into a new quagmire of pseudo-knowledge. In that case truth will be served up in such an indigestible and vague form that it produces the impression of a pathological delirium. He will be shown ways and means of developing hidden powers and capacities which he is promised, if he is persistent, will without much trouble give him power and domain over everything, including animate creatures, inert matter and the elements. All these systems, based on a variety of theories, are extraordinarily alluring, no doubt precisely because of their vagueness. They have a particular attraction for the half-educated, those who are half-instructed in positivist knowledge.

In view of the fact that most questions studied from the point of view of esoteric and occult theories often go beyond the limits of data accessible to modern science, these theories often look down on it. Although on the one hand they give positivist science its due, on the other, they belittle its importance and leave the impression that science is not only a failure but even worse.

What is the use then of going to the university, of studying and straining over official textbooks, if theories of this kind enable one to look down on all other learning and to pass judgment on scientific questions?

But there is one important thing the study of such theories does not give; it does not engender objectivity in questions of knowledge, less so even than science. Indeed it tends to blur a man's brain and to diminish his capacity for reasoning and thinking soundly, and leads him toward psychopathy. This is the effect of such theories on the half-educated who take them for authentic revelation. But their effect is not very different on scientists themselves, who may have been affected, however slightly, by the poison of discontent with existing things. Our thinking machine possesses the capacity to be convinced of anything you like, provided it is repeatedly and persistently influenced in the required direction. A thing that may appear absurd to start with will in the end become rationalized, provided it is repeated sufficiently often and with sufficient conviction. And, just as one type will repeat ready-made words which have stuck in his mind, so a second type will find intricate proofs and paradoxes to explain what he says. But both are equally to be pitied. All these theories offer assertions which, like dogmas, usually cannot be verified. Or in any case they cannot be verified by the means available to us.

Then methods and ways of self-development are suggested which are said to lead to a state in which their assertions can be verified. There can be no objection to this in principle. But the consistent practice of these methods may lead the overzealous seeker to highly undesirable results. A man who accepts occult theories and believes himself knowledgeable in this sphere will not be able to resist the temptation to put into practice the knowledge of the methods he has gained in his research, that is, he will pass from knowledge to action. Perhaps he will act with circumspection, avoiding methods which from his point of view are risky, and applying the more reliable and authentic ways; perhaps he will observe with the greatest of care. All the same, the temptation to apply them and the insistence on the necessity for doing so, as well as the emphasis laid on the miraculous nature of the results and the concealment of their dark sides, will lead a man to try them.

Perhaps, in trying them, a man will find methods which are harmless for him. Perhaps, in applying them, he will even get something from them. In general, all the methods for self-development which are offered, whether for verification, as a means, or as an end, are often contradictory and incomprehensible. Dealing as they do with such an intricate, little-known machine as the human organism and with that side of our life closely connected with it which we call our psyche, the least mistake in carrying them out, the smallest error or excess of pressure can lead to irreparable damage to the machine.

It is indeed lucky if a man escapes from this morass more or less intact. Unfortunately very many of those who are engaged in the development of spiritual powers and capacities end their career in a lunatic asylum or ruin their health and psyche to such a degree that they become complete invalids, unable to adapt to life. Their ranks are swelled by those who are attracted to pseudo-occultism out of a longing for anything miraculous and mysterious. There are also those exceptionally weak-willed individuals who are failures in life and who, out of considerations of personal gain, dream of developing in themselves the power and the ability to subjugate others. And finally there are people who are simply looking for variety in life, for ways of forgetting their sorrows, of finding distraction from the boredom of the daily round and of escaping its conflicts.

As their hopes of attaining the qualities they counted on begin to dwindle, it is easy for them to fall into intentional charlatanism. I remember a classic example. A certain seeker after psychic power, a man who was well off, well read, who had traveled widely in his search for anything miraculous, ended by going bankrupt and became at the same time disillusioned in all his researches.

Looking for another means of livelihood, he hit on the idea of making use of the pseudo-knowledge on which he had spent so much money and energy. No sooner said than done. He wrote a book, bearing one of those titles that adorn the covers of occult books, something like *A Course in Development of the Hidden Forces in Man*.

This course was written in seven lectures and represented a short encyclopedia of secret methods for developing magnetism, hypnotism, telepathy, clairvoyance, clairaudience, escape into the astral realm, levitation and other alluring capacities. The course was well advertised, put on sale at an exceedingly high price, although in the end an appreciable discount (up to 95 percent) was offered to the more persistent or parsimonious customers on condition that they recommend it to their friends.

Owing to the general interest in such

matters, the success of the course exceeded all the expectations of its compiler. Soon he began to receive letters from purchasers in enthusiastic, reverent and deferential tones, addressing him as "dear teacher" and "wise mentor" and expressing deepest gratitude for the wonderful exposition and most valuable instruction which gave them the possibility of developing various occult capacities remarkably quickly.

These letters made a considerable collection and each of them surprised him until there at last came a letter informing him that with the help of his course someone had, in about a month, become able to levitate. This indeed overran the cup of his astonishment.

Here are his actual words: "I am astonished at the absurdity of things that happen. I, who wrote the course, have no very clear idea of the nature of the phenomena I am teaching. Yet these idiots not only find their way about in this gibberish but even learn something from it and now some superidiot has even learned to fly. It is, of course, all nonsense. He can go to hell.... Soon they will put him into a straitjacket. It will serve him right. We are much better off without such fools."

Occultists, do you appreciate the argument of this author of one of the textbooks on psychodevelopment? In this case, it is possible that somebody might accidentally learn something, for often a man, though ignorant himself, can speak with curious correctness about various things, without knowing how he does it. At the same time, of course, he also talks such nonsense that any truths he may have expressed are completely buried and it is utterly impossible to dig the pearl of truth out of the muckheap of every kind of nonsense.

"Why this strange capacity?" you may ask. The reason is very simple. As I have already said, we have no knowledge of our own, that is, knowledge given by life itself, knowledge that cannot be taken away from us. All our knowledge, which is merely information, may be valuable or worthless. In absorbing it like a sponge, we can easily repeat and talk about it logically and convincingly, while understanding nothing about it. It is equally easy for us to lose it, for it is not ours but has been poured into us like some liquid poured into a vessel. Crumbs of truth are scattered everywhere; and those who know and understand can see and marvel how close people live to the truth, yet how blind they are and how powerless to penetrate it. But in searching for it, it is far better not to venture at all into the dark labyrinths of human stupidity and ignorance than to go there alone. For without the guidance and explanations of someone who knows, a man at every step, without noticing it, may suffer a strain, a dislocation of his machine, after which he would have to spend a great deal more on its repair than he spent damaging it.

What can you think of a solid individual who says of himself that "he is a man of perfect meekness and that his behavior is not under the jurisdiction of those around him, since he lives on a mental plane to which standards of physical life cannot be applied"?

Actually, his behavior should long ago have been the subject of study by a psychiatrist. This is a man who conscientiously and persistently "works" on himself for hours daily, that is, he applies all his efforts to deepening and strengthening further the psychological twist, which is already so serious that I am convinced that he will soon be in an insane asylum.

I could quote hundreds of examples of wrongly directed search and where it leads. I could tell you the names of well-known people in public life who have become deranged through occultism and who live in our midst and astonish us by their eccentricities. I could tell you the exact method that deranged them, in what realm they "worked" and "developed" themselves and how these affected their psychological makeup and why.

But this question could form the subject of a long and separate conversation so, for lack of time, I will not permit myself to dwell on it now.

The more a man studies the obstacles and deceptions which lie in wait for him at every step in this realm, the more convinced he becomes that it is impossible to travel the path of self-development on the chance instructions of chance people, or the kind of information culled from reading and casual talk.

At the same time he gradually sees more clearly—first a feeble glimmer, then the clear light of truth which has illumined mankind throughout the ages. The beginnings of initiation are lost in the darkness of time, where the long chain of epochs unfolds. Great cultures and civilizations loom up, dimly arising from cults and mysteries, ever changing, disappearing and reappearing.

The Great Knowledge is handed on in succession from age to age, from people to people, from race to race. The great centers of initiation in India, Assyria, Egypt, Greece, illumine the world with a bright light. The revered names of the great initiates, the living bearers of the truth, are handed on reverently from generation to generation. Truth is fixed by means of symbolic writings and legends and is transmitted to the mass of people for preservation in the form of customs and ceremonies, in oral traditions, in memorials, in sacred art through the invisible quality in dance, music, sculpture and various rituals. It is communicated openly after a definite trial to those who seek it and is preserved by oral transmission in the chain of those who know. After a certain time has elapsed, the centers of initiation die out one after another, and the ancient knowledge departs through underground channels into the deep, hiding from the eyes of the seekers.

The bearers of this knowledge also hide, becoming unknown to those around them, but they do not cease to exist. From time to time separate streams break through to the surface, showing that somewhere deep down in the interior, even in our day, there flows the powerful ancient stream of true knowledge of being.

To break through to this stream, to find it —this is the task and the aim of the search;

for, having found it, a man can entrust himself boldly to the way by which he intends to go; then there only remains "to know" in order "to be" and "to do." On this way a man will not be entirely alone; at difficult moments he will receive support and guidance, for all who follow this way are connected by an uninterrupted chain.

Perhaps the only positive result of all wanderings in the windings paths and tracks of occult research will be that, if a man preserves the capacity for sound judgment and thought, he will evolve that special faculty of discrimination which can be called flair. He will discard the ways of psychopathy and error and will persistently search for true ways. And here, as in self-knowledge, the principle which I have already quoted holds good: "In order to do it, it is necessary to know; but in order to know, it is necessary to find out how to know."

To a man who is searching with all his being, with all his inner self, comes the unfailing conviction that to find out how to know in order to do is possible only by finding a guide with experience and knowledge, who will take on his spiritual guidance and become his teacher.

And it is here that a man's flair is more important than anywhere else. He chooses a guide for himself. It is of course an indispensable condition that he choose as a guide a man who knows, or else all meaning of choice is lost. Who can tell where a guide who does not know may lead a man?

Every seeker dreams of a guide who knows, dreams about him but seldom asks himself objectively and sincerely—is he worthy of being guided? Is he ready to follow the way?

Go out one clear starlit night to some open space and look up at the sky, at those millions of worlds over your head. Remember that perhaps on each of them swarm billions of beings, similar to you or perhaps superior to you in their organization. Look at the Milky Way. The earth cannot even be called a grain of sand in this infinity. It dissolves and vanishes, and with it, you. Where are you? And is what you want simply madness?

Before all these worlds ask yourself what are your aims and hopes, your intentions and means of fulfilling them, the demands that may be made upon you and your preparedness to meet them.

A long and difficult journey is before you; you are preparing for a strange and unknown land. The way is infinitely long. You do not know if rest will be possible on the way nor where it will be possible. You should be prepared for the worst. Take all the necessities for the journey with you.

Try to forget nothing, for afterwards it will be too late and there will be no time to go back for what has been forgotten, to rectify the mistake. Weigh up your strength. Is it sufficient for the whole journey? How soon can you start?

Remember that if you spend longer on the way you will need to carry proportionately more supplies, and this will delay you further both on the way and in your preparations for it. Yet every minute is precious. Once having decided to go, there is no use wasting time.

Do not reckon on trying to come back. This experiment may cost you very dear. The guide undertakes only to take you there and, if you wish to turn back, he is not obliged to return with you. You will be left to yourself, and woe to you if you weaken or forget the way—you will never get back. And even if you remember the way, the question still remains—will you return safe and sound? For many unpleasantnesses await the lonely traveler who is not familiar with the way and the customs which prevail there. Bear in mind that your sight has the property of presenting distant objects as though they were near. Beguiled by the nearness of the aim toward which you strive, blinded by its beauty and ignorant of the measure of your own strength, you will not notice the obstacles on the way; you will not see the numerous ditches across the path. In a green meadow covered with luxuriant flowers, in the thick grass, a deep precipice is hidden. It is very easy to stumble and fall over it if your eyes are not concentrated on the step you are taking.

Do not forget to concentrate all your attention on the nearest sector of the way—do not concern yourself about far aims if you do not wish to fall over the precipice.

Yet do not forget your aim. Remember it the whole time and keep up in yourself an active endeavor toward it, so as not to lose the right direction. And once you have started, be observant; what you have passed through remains behind and will not appear again; so if you fail to notice it at the time, you never will notice it.

Do not be overcurious nor waste time on things that attract your attention but are not worth it. Time is precious and should not be wasted on things which have no direct relation to your aim.

Remember where you are and why you are here.

Do not protect yourselves and remember that no effort is made in vain.

And now you can set out on the way.

Essentuki, About 1918

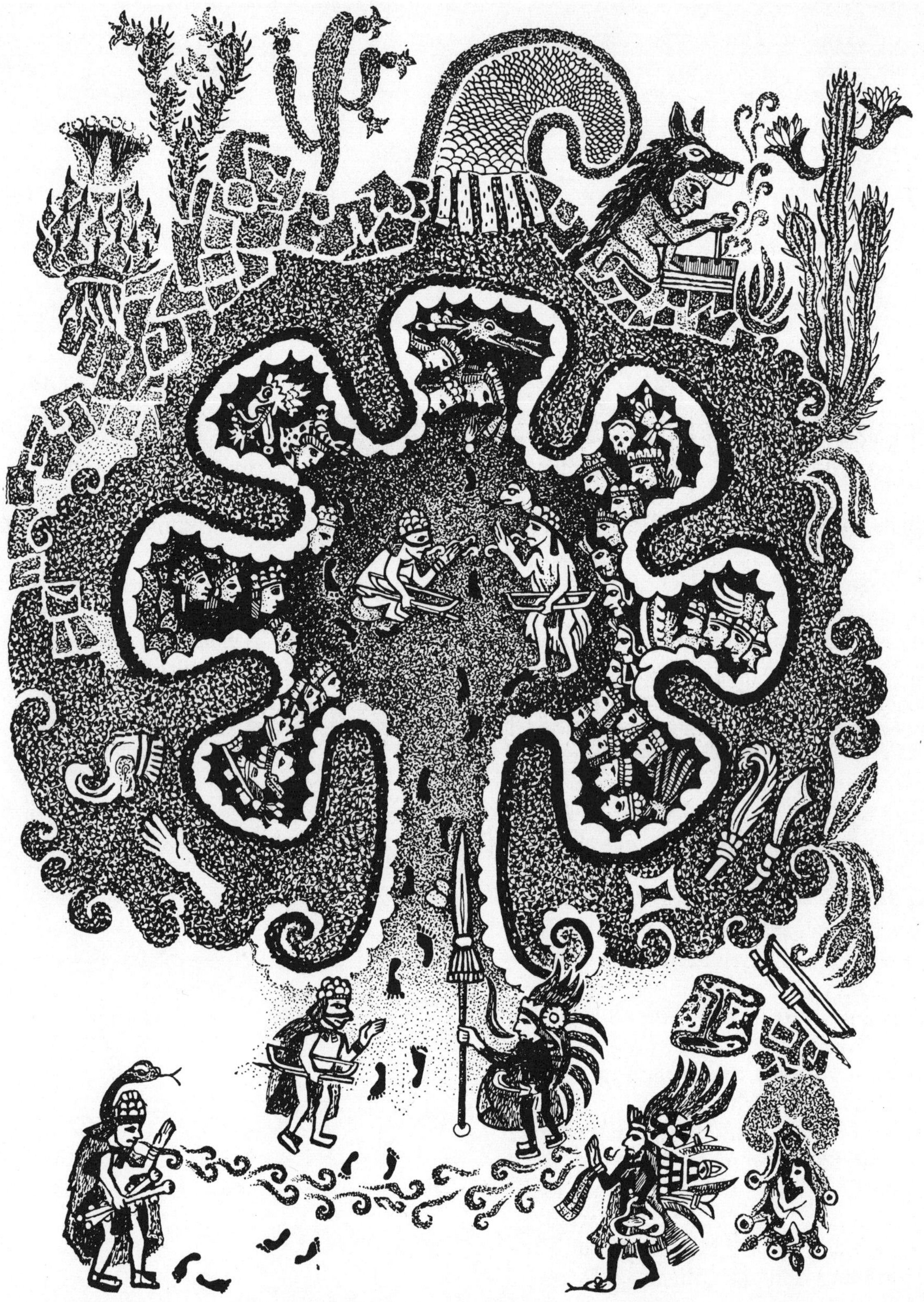

Toward Climax

Gary Snyder

I.

salt seas, mountains, deserts
cell mandala holding water
nerve network linking toes and eyes
fins   legs   wings—
teeth, all purpose little early mammal molars.
primate flat-foot
front fore–mounted eyes—

watching at the forest-grassland (interface
richness) edge.
scavenge, gather, rise up on rear legs.
running—grasping—hand and eye;
hunting.
calling others to the stalk, the drive.

note sharp points of split bone, the broken rock.

brain–size blossoming out
on the balance of the neck,
tough skin—good eyes—sharp ears—
move in bands.
milkweed fiber rolled out on the thigh
    nets to carry fruits or meat.

catch fire, move out.
eurasia tundra reindeer herds
sewn hide clothing, mammoth-rib-framework tent.

Bison, bear
    opening animal chests and bellies, skulls,
      bodies just like ours—
pictures in caves.
send sound off the mouth and lips
formal complex grammars transect
    inner structures & the daily world—

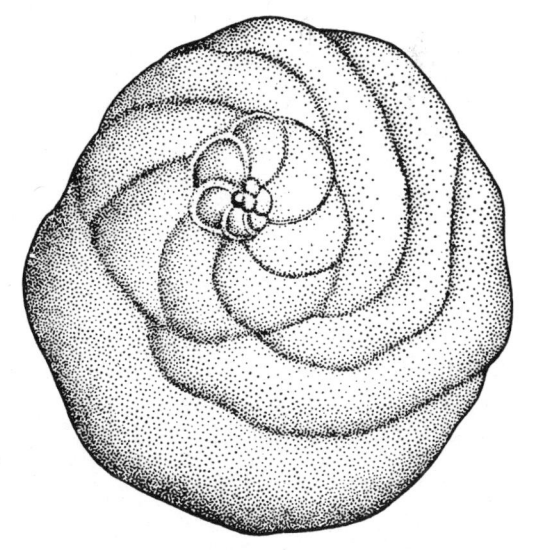

big herds dwindle
    (—did we kill them?
    thousand-mile front of prairie fire—)
ice age warms up
learn more plants. netting, trapping, boats.
bow and arrow. dogs.
mingle bands and families in and out like language
    kin to grubs and trees and wolves

    dance and sing
begin to go "beyond"—reed flute
    buried baby wrapped in many furs—
great dream-time tales to tell.

squash blossom in the garbage heap.
    start farming.
cows won't stay away, start herding.
weaving, throwing clay.
get better off, get class,
make lists, start writing down.

    forget wild plants, their virtues
    lose dream-time
    lose largest size of brain—

get safer, tighter, wrapped in,
winding smaller, spreading wider,
lay towns out in streets in rows,
and build a wall.

drain swamp for wet-rice grasses, burn back woods,
herd men like cows.
have slaves build a fleet
raid for wealth—bronze weapons:
study stars and figure central
never-moving Pole Star King.

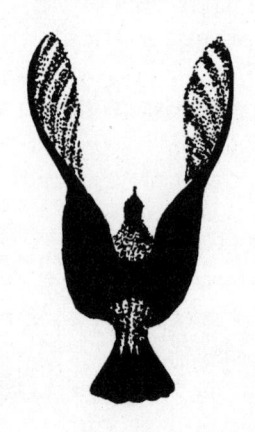

II.

From "King" project a Law. (Foxy self-survival sense is Reason, since it "works") and Reason gets ferocious as it goes for order throughout nature—turns Law back on nature. (A rooster was burned at the stake for laying an egg. Unnatural. 1474.)

III.

science walks in beauty:

nets are many knots
skin is border-guard, a pelt is borrowed warmth;
a bow is the flex of a limb in the wind
a giant downtown building
    is a creekbed stood on end.

detritus pathways. "delayed and complex ways
to pass the food through webs."

maturity. stop and think. draw on the mind's
stored richness. memory, dream, half-digested
image of your life. "detritus pathways"—feed
the many tiny things that feed an owl.
send heart boldly travelling,
on the heat of the dead & down.

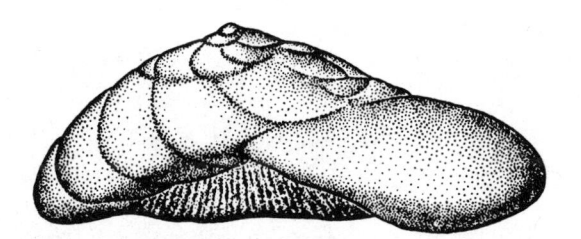

IV.

two logging songs

Clear-cut

Forestry. "How
Many people
Were harvested
In Viet-Nam?"

Clear-cut. "Some
Were children.
Some were over-ripe."

Virgin

A virgin
Forest
Is ancient; many-
Breasted,
Stable; at
Climax.

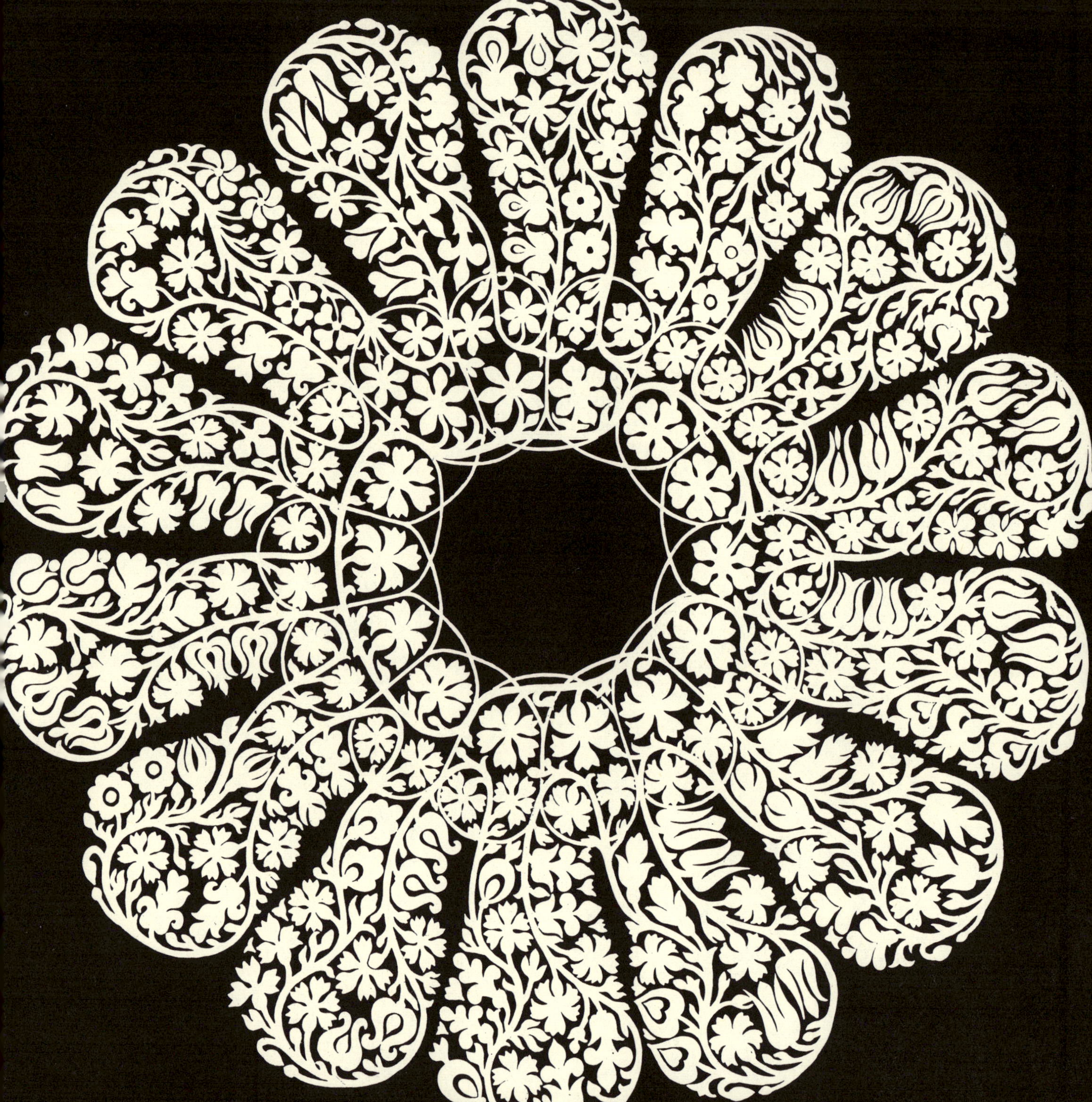

Patterns of Greater Reality

George Doczi

Coded Patterns

According to the Pali Canon the Buddha once gave a sermon without saying a word. He merely held up a flower to his listeners in utter silence. This was the famous "Flower Sermon."

Every flower is a sermon without words. It speaks about unfolding from a center and about much more. But it speaks in the code-language of patterns and a key is needed to decipher this code. Proportions furnish such a key because *proportions are relationships* of parts and whole, and every pattern is made up of such relationships. Based upon this consideration all kinds of patterns can be compared with each other, yielding sometimes quite unexpected results.

The following design studies compare proportional patterns of a daisy, a human body, a dream, a poem, a pine cone, a galaxy and waves of water. These comparisons point in one direction: towards the *relatedness of all things*.

Awareness of such relatedness is as old as mankind. We have archaic man's testimony enshrined in the words of the American Indian sage Black Elk: "It is only the ignorant person who sees many where there is really only one." We have the words of the Upanishads which preceded the Buddha: "Tat tvam asi. That art thou."

Through the centuries this ancient truth had been forgotten and buried in Western man's exultant effort to become the conqueror and master of nature. Now, when the dangerous futility of such conceit is brought home—not in the least through ecological disasters—the ancient truth reappears again. It shows man to set his sight not upon conquest and mastery but upon *proper relations* with nature—and with his fellow beings. That there *are* such *proper* relations is the basic message of the patterns of nature.

This message reveals that something wants to unfold in man like a flower, like a sunburst. It also *demonstrates* that man is not alone in a hostile universe, but related to wildflower, wind and water, related to the "four-legged, two-legged, and winged ones" and related even to those nameless ones, which struggle to be born from the darkness and light of a Greater Reality, which is all about and within every human being.

Such recognitions signal the beginnings of a new age, born from the awareness of the responsibility and joy of being human. These design studies confirm this responsibility, they celebrate this joy.

DAISY AND HUMAN BODY

Figure 1 is a diagrammatic representation of the center of a daisy. Each floret is represented by a circle. The drawing shows that the florets grow at the meeting-points of two sets of spirals that evolve from the same center in opposite directions, one clockwise, the other counterclockwise. One pair of these opposing spirals is marked separately in diagram A.

The fact that the spirals move in *opposite* directions and that it is their *joint* action which determines the design makes this one more instance of the joining complementary opposites so frequently met with in nature. (Day and night, female and male, positive and negative electricity, etc.)

One can reconstruct this design the same

Figure 1

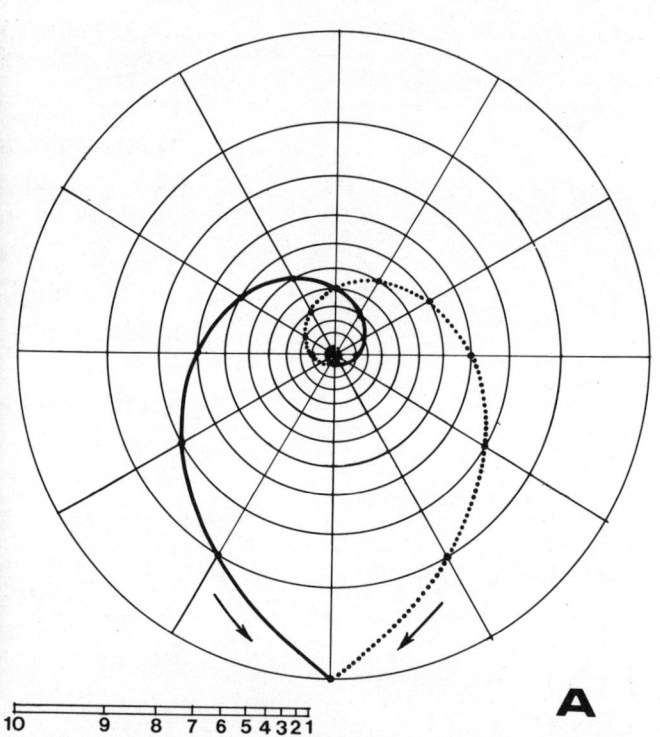

A

way this diagram was made, by drawing a set of concentric circles (at distances that grow in a logarithmic rate from the center) and intersecting these circles with a series of straight lines, equidistant from the same center. Consecutive meeting points of these two sets of lines, when connected, furnish the spirals. This reconstruction method itself is an instance of the joint action of the complementary opposites, since the round and straight lines here again form a pair of opposites, which unite, cooperate or act in *synergy*.

This *synergy of opposites* manifests itself also in the design of the human body, as Leonardo da Vinci's famous study of a mature man's body indicates (Figure 2). Leonardo drew both a circle and a square around this figure to illustrate his observation that in a full grown man's body the extended extremities touch both opposites: the round (circle) and the straight-angled (square), both centered on the navel. The navel is the central point from which the body once unfolded, as the daisy unfolds from its own center.

These two designs have a further characteristic in common: there is an order of proportional relationships operating in both, which proves to be the same in both cases, in spite of the difference in shapes. The bar-diagrams drawn alongside this man's figure and repeated in the triangular composite-diagram at the right show that the length of the members of this body relate to each other and to the whole body in a unique way. The smaller of two neighboring members always has a tendency to relate to the larger in the

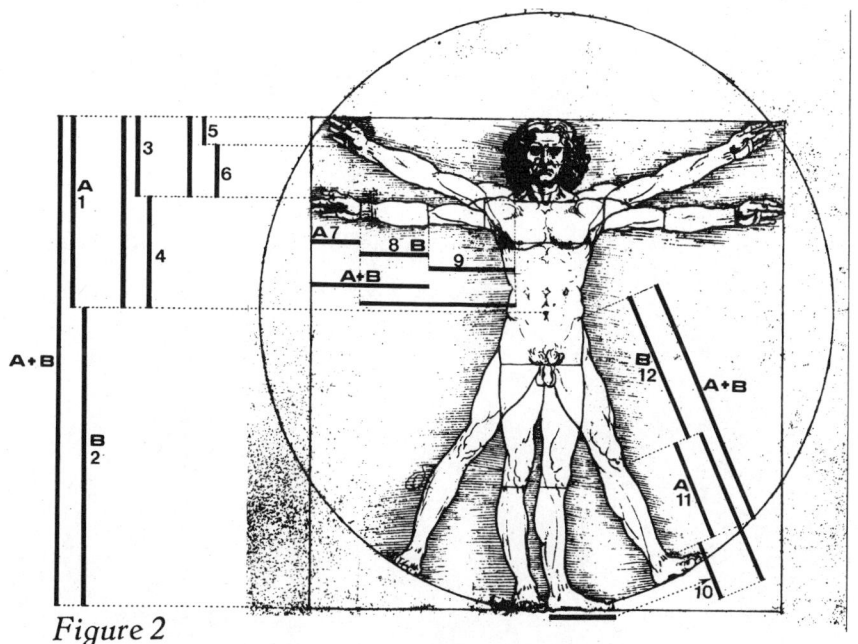

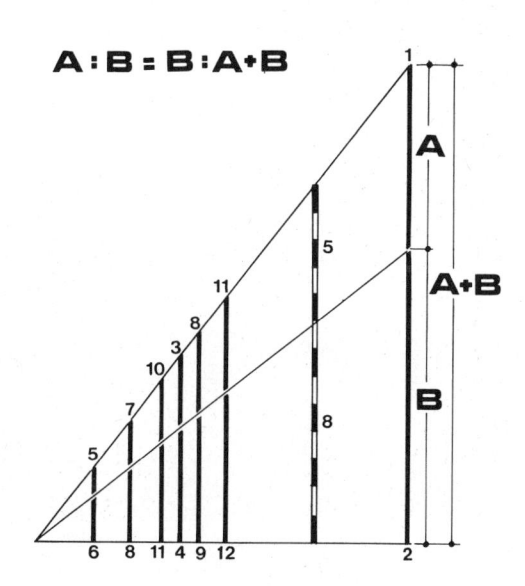

Figure 2

77

same way as the larger relates to both of them joined together. Expressed in equation form: A stands to B as B stands to A + B. The biologist C. H. Waddington refers to this as the "Relatedness of Neighbors."

In literature this proportion is mostly referred to as the "Golden Section" (or "Golden Proportion"), since there is only *one* such point on any given line that will bisect it in this *unique* way.

Among numbers the lowest integers which relate this way are 5 and 8, because $5:8 = 0.62$, and $8:(5+8)$ or 13 also equals 0.62. The actual ratio of the Golden Proportion is really 0.618..., the three dots indicating that this is an irrational number, so called because it never can be expressed *fully* as a ratio of whole numbers, it can only be approximated; larger numbers standing in this proportion can be divided and divided without end. *Infinity* thus enters the rational world with this proportion; an alarming entry which so frightened the Greeks when they discovered it that they kept it a closely guarded secret, with the death penalty imposed upon those who would dare reveal it. Basic to this proportion is the *shared* relationship, or ratio between all the large and small parts of a whole. This shared relationship curtails the growth of each member within the discipline of definite limits, but in return it makes each a participant in the greater, pulsating rhythm of the *whole* body, transforming its *many parts* of the most varied shapes and sizes into *one integrated unity of wholeness*. Because of its *transforming power* this proportion has also

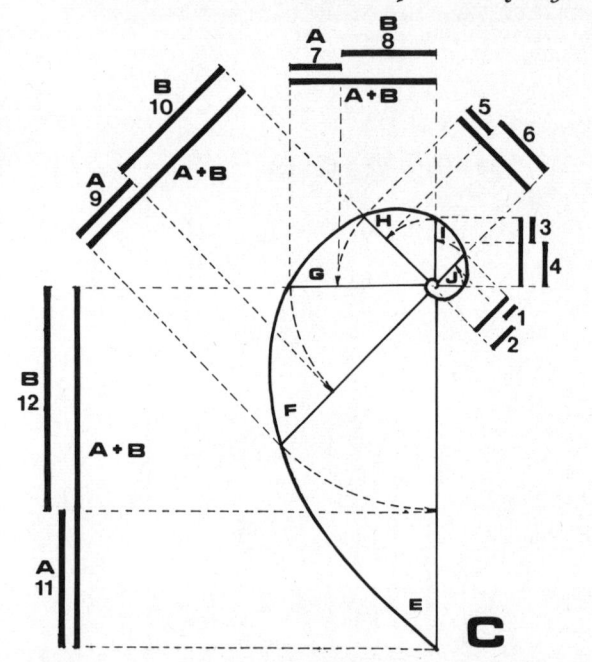

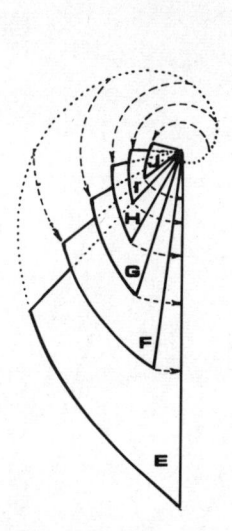

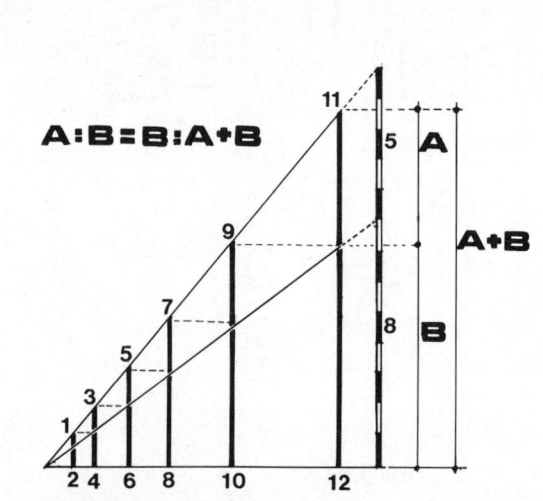

Figure 3

been referred to as "divine" and frequently applied in great works of art and architecture. There are other, similar proportions but none is so frequent as this one, and none possesses this uniqueness. It is the proportion most frequently encountered in the designs of organic nature.

Leonardo da Vinci summed up the significance of this unique proportional relationship in the following words: "Every part is disposed to unite with the whole, that it may thereby escape from its incompleteness."

The design of the daisy shows that a similar relationship governs its development. This can be demonstrated by segments representing successive stages of the evolution of the spirals. These segments can be rotated around the center of the daisy until they completely overlap like a folded fan, proving that they all have the same proportions (Figure 3B). Diagrams C and D of Figure 3 show that growth proceeds from one stage to the next according to the same golden proportional discipline of the "Relatedness of Neighbors" observed in the design of the human body. Since the spirals represent successive stages of growth, and they remain true to their proportions throughout the entire development, one can say that such patterns are patterns of *selftrue* proportional relations.

This cursory comparison of the design patterns of human body and daisy reveals that they share certain basic patterning processes. This accord—summed up and translated from the code-language of patterns—seems to indicate that *unfolding from a center, synergy of opposites* and *selftrue proportional relations* are basic features of organic development.

Since such patterning principles hold true in many physical instances it seems that they may also apply on other levels of experience. This idea is close at hand considering the interrelatedness and mutual interdependence of the physical and psychic worlds. Theoretical physics and psychosomatic medicine alike agree that body and soul, or matter and mind, are two aspects of the same phenomenon, like two ends of the same stick. The depth-psychology of C. G. Jung and his followers is particularly rich in observations of parallels between physical and psychic processes, including the above mentioned ones.

PROPORTIONS OF A NIGHTMARE

Perhaps the example of a dream can demonstrate how the above patterning processes are at work in shaping not only the physical body, but also the inner world of man.

Figure 4 records successive stages of a nightmare which I had myself, at the time when the late Italian dictator was at the height of his power. I hated him: he and his likes forged the dictatorships which brought about the second world war, swallowing up so many, and making so many more into homeless fugitives, including myself. When I made these drawings I needed to study the facial expressions in detail, so for lack of a better model I mimicked for myself in front of a mirror. Only after the drawings were completed did I realize—and it came as a shock to me—that the hated dictator's face had become my own face!

Did this mean that I, the ardent opponent of all dictatorships, the powerless victim of their power, also had such a dictator within me: an unrecognized drive for power, the exact opposite of all that I stood for in my waking, conscious life? Yes, I had to admit that the truth was something like that. Life-energy, my striving for accomplishment, for relationships, for recognition was not being realized in my waking life. And it was this unlived part of my life that demanded recognition, by tormenting me with such nightmares! Yes, here was my *opposite*, the shadow Jung speaks about, and it was no good to turn against him in rage and disgust, to condemn him with fury, or to run away from him in fear. He was disguised as the Italian dictator, but in reality he was a part of myself, a part that was not related to the whole, because it was unrealized, unrecognized and unaccepted. Only by facing this part of me, and by bringing it into *selftrue* relations with the other, conscious parts of my psyche could it be integrated into the wholeness pattern of a fuller life. Only so could it be transformed from a devouring, *destructive* monster into a *creative* power, turning *his* inner sword into *my* ploughshare.

The frightening emotional impact of such nightmares indicates an urgent need for synergy of the opposites. The giant size of the

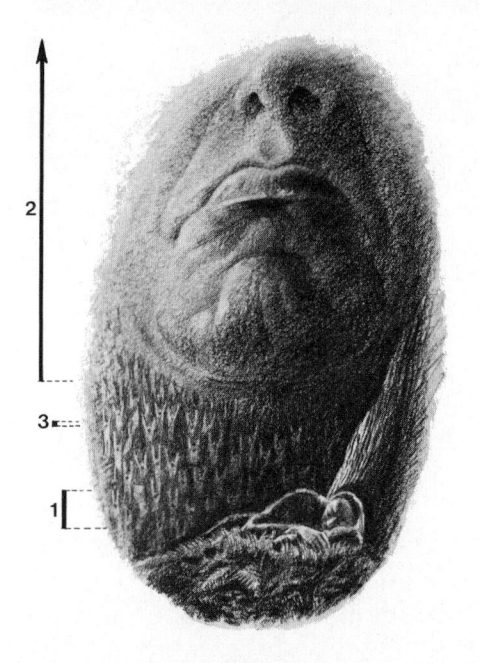

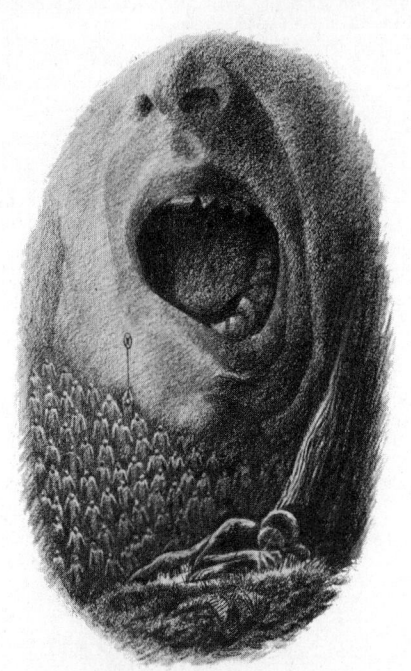

Figure 4

devouring dictator, inflated beyond all proportions reveals the dangerous degree of disproportions existing here. These disproportions are demonstrated by the bar diagrams at the left, which show no proportional relationships whatever between each other. 1) represents the dreamer's conscious ego, as known to himself. 2) is his enormous unconscious opposite or shadow. 3) is one of the dreamer's unrealized potentials, which present themselves here as midgets, huddled in a gray, undifferentiated mass, like unhatched fisheggs, galvanized by the monster's voice and wiggling like worms to escape being devoured.

These are snapshots of an inner scene, as any dreams are. They show that even the psyche has its own proportions, like the body. Nightmares are warning signals of a lack of selftrue proportions between the conscious and unconscious parts of the psyche. Happy dreams are often encouraging signs, indicating that such relations are in progress of being realized.

Of course not every dream can be readily illustrated with bar diagrams. But every dreamer sooner or later encounters the disguised opposites in his or her dreams, which signal—by the magnitude and intensity of their emotional impact—a need for changed inner relationships. In this striving, the connected conscious and unconscious parts of the psyche do act like the neighboring members of the body: they strive for more selftrue relations with each other and with the wholeness of the individual, "that they may thereby escape from their incompleteness." *A dream is part of the body of the soul.*

Dream patterns when decoded reveal not only the unconscious motives or unknown parts of the psyche, they also indicate the directions in which the conscious ego must go to realize the wholeness pattern of the full grown personality. This nightmare shows the ego prostrate and completely "overshadowed" by its monstrous opponent, indicating this ego's need to claim some of the surplus power being usurped by its overblown, tyrannical opponent. Only by a disciplined conscious effort of the ego could more selftrue inner relationships be established. Only so could the fishegg-midgets be hatched and transformed into fulfilled potentials.

And yet the ego is *not* the center of its own development. The self-regulating evolutionary process which is trying to unfold often more fully than circumstances would permit—or the conscious ego could imagine or dare to hope for—emanates from a hidden, creative inner center, which is not the center of egocentricity. This hidden creative center is the navel of the soul: it is the point at which the soul was once attached to the womb of a Greater Reality, from which it was born and received its first nourishment. The patterns of life continue to unfold from the depth of this creative center, like the spirals unfold from the center of the daisy. And just like these spirals continue to be nourished by Mother Earth, so does the soul continue to receive its nourishment from Greater Reality in ways that are not visible to the naked eye.

However, the realization that the ego is not the center of its own unfolding does not reduce the ego's significance. Quite to the contrary: only so can the ego *relate* to Greater Reality. This dream pattern could not have been decoded without a disciplined and sustained ego-effort to understand it, including the making of these drawings. A dream is a challenge to the ego, coming as it does come from the depth of the creative center. It does require the ego's *creative response* to accomplish its task. This task is the full development, the growth and maturing of the dreamer through the constant *transformations* of life, towards greater wholeness, greater health, Greater Reality.

Figure 5A

A Mandala of Sonnets

It has been often recognized that the body-social of mankind also has its dreams, which take shape in works of art and poetry. Some poems certainly reveal patterning processes similar to the ones which shape the dreams of the individual. This may be especially true when social conditions prevent the development of selftrue relationships within society and within the individual.

In 1923 an eighteen year old Hungarian, Attila József wrote a set of fifteen sonnets which are such dream-poems. All the previously discussed patterning processes are clearly recognizable in these sonnets, which are jointly called "Songs of the Cosmos." They are composed along the lines of the "Sonetti Corona" of the Italian Renaissance, according to the following pattern: the last line of every sonnet is also the first line of the following sonnet, and the last line of the last sonnet is identical with the first line of the first sonnet. There is also a fifteenth or master-sonnet, which consists of nothing but the first lines of all fourteen preceding sonnets combined in consecutive order, and so that they convey a summary statement of the basic message of the entire work. Following is my translation of this master-sonnet.

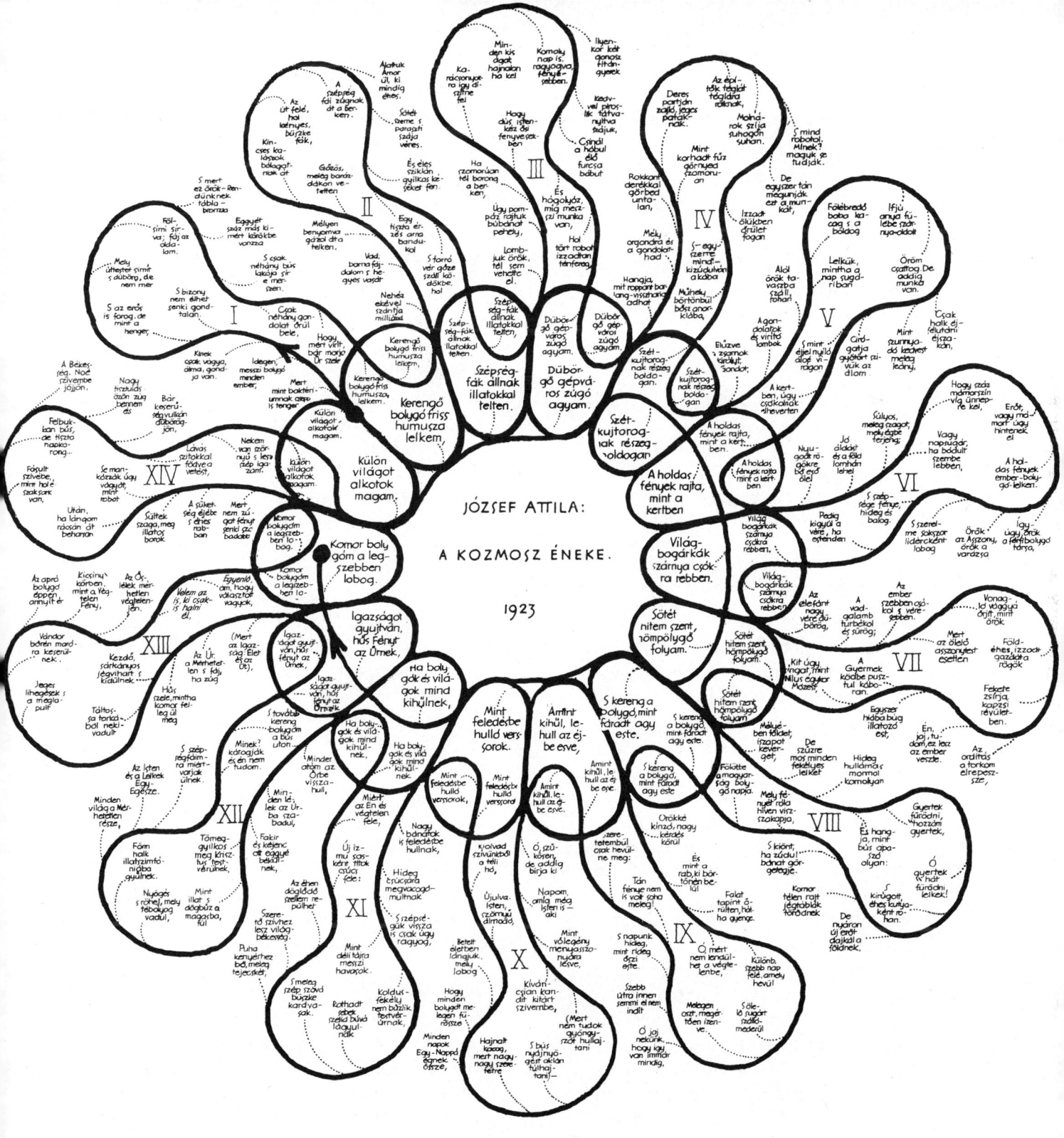

Figure 5B

I am a world all by myself alone,
my soul is fresh soil of a spinning planet's sphere.
Trees of beauty full of fragrance flourish here,
my brain: a city filled with motor-drone.

Moonlight patches, tipsy drunkards quiver
in my lune-lit grove, like in a dark garden.
Worlds wing by like bugs, to mate-dance in the glen
over my dark faith: my sacred river.

My planet spins as my worn brain does at night,
it cools off and falls, disappearing from light,
like lines of poems, forgotten in my youth.

If all the worlds and all planets shall turn cold
one cool light shall flare up in the void most bold
kindled by the blaze of my lone planet's truth.

Figure 5A is a pictorial image of the word-mandala of these fifteen sonnets. In this pattern, motifs taken from Hungarian folk-art are substituted for the words of the sonnets. Every flower stands for a line, each loop represents a sonnet. The windings of the vine indicate the stanzas of each sonnet: two quatrains followed by two terzets. The central garland represents the master-sonnet.

The pattern demonstrates that all fifteen sonnets (Figure 5B) are interwoven into a single, harmonious whole, in which all parts are *related* to each other and to the whole by one shared relationship, while maintaining their own identity, corresponding to the *selftrue* relations of the patterns discussed earlier. This *relatedness* of all parts of the pattern is in sharp contrast to the *unrelatedness* of the lonely planet, to which the young poet likens his soul, as it orbits in outer space "seared by Winds of Void," a word image which only too accurately depicts his actual life situation. He was a child of poverty, to whom even some of the most basic human relationships of love and care were denied in earliest childhood, both by society and by his personal fate: he never knew his father, and he grew up on the streets. But the youth did not surrender to these challenges of life. He faced them and he struggled with them, knowing that—in spite of the miserable, petty reality of his days—a Greater Reality belonged to him by birthright, as it does to all human beings.

In the agony of his loneliness—his personal and social unrelatedness—he reached out for the discipline of an age-old artform, in which every part *is* related to every other part and to whole, as branches and leaves are related to the trunk of a tree. And along these branches the vine of his song rose and ripened. In the graphic pattern one can follow these vines as they unfold from the central garland of the master-sonnet, rhyme by rhyme, stanza by stanza, sonnet by sonnet until the whole pattern of the song is complete, and the last line had indeed become the first line. Here is transformation, synergy of opposites and unfolding from the center all in one.

PINE CONE AND GALAXY
Creativity is such a great word that it is often abused, so that it is sometimes difficult to know what is meant by it. The mandala pattern of the Song of the Cosmos demonstrates one specific aspect of creativity as the

responsible response to the challenges of life; responsible because it faces and shoulders the burden of the synergic opposites, struggling for transformation and wholeness. The nightmare pattern showed a similar, creative transformation process at work in the dreamer's psyche, intent upon growth and the unfolding of potentials through establishment of more selftrue proportional relations between the "known" ego and the "unknown" shadow.

The patterns of the human body and the daisy are likewise patterns of creative transformation in this sense: they also grow from the union of synergic opposites according to selftrue proportions. Figure 6 demonstrates that pine cones too develop in such creative patterns (along with a very large number of other species of the plant and animal kingdoms). However, the pine cone's spirals do not remain in one plane as those of the daisy, but rise along the center-line of the cone, as around a spindle, thus becoming three-dimensional helixes. The plan-projection of these helixes is a reminder of patterns of some galaxies.

The sense of wonder and awe which some of these patterns convey derives from the sudden confrontation with energies and orders that come from an entirely different center than the ego's and that are nevertheless also within the individual human being.

"Each one of us is a focal point, at which energies that pass our understanding meet and function." Since energies, such as these are beyond the capacities of rational thinking to grasp, they have often been referred to as

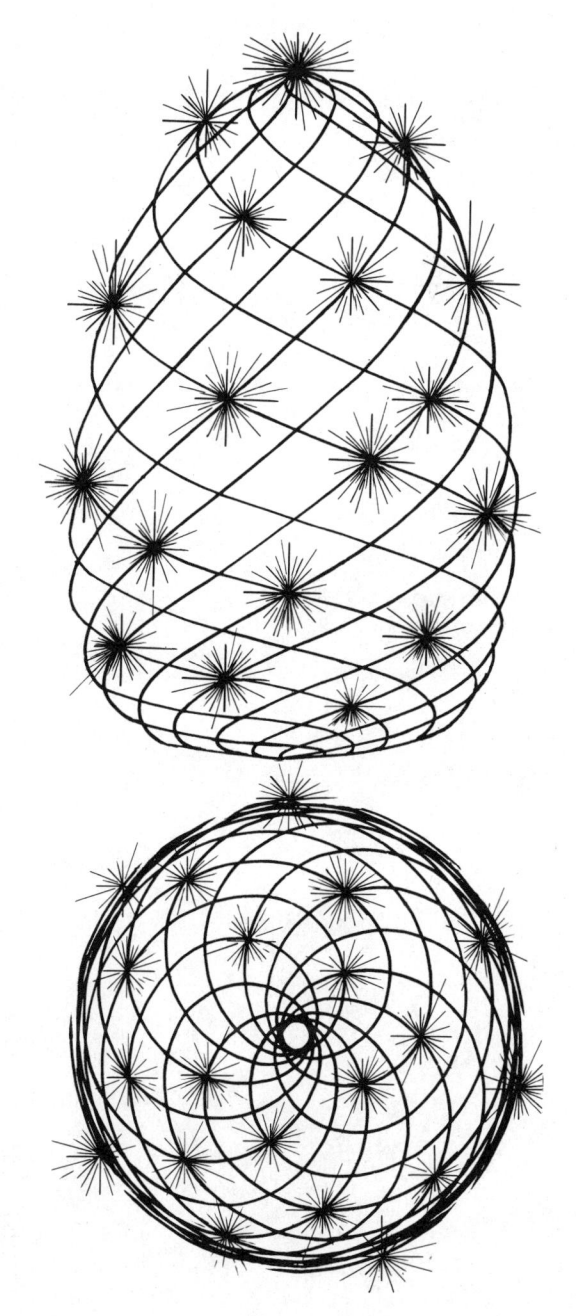

Figure 6

Figure 7

"divine" and recorded as such in mythology and religious poetry. The story of the burning bush and the wrestling with the unknown opponent in the Bible, as well as many experiences of the mystics are some examples. But religion has no sole claim upon this experience. Every child which blows away the seeds of a dandelion senses it, every lover who has ever looked into the eyes of the beloved knows it. Since the essence of this experience is the realization of a compelling power, greater than that of the individual's ego it has been called *numinous*,—an adjective derived from the Latin "numen" which originally meant a nod from a divine being, a nod of compelling power.

Thus a further decoded message of patterns says that the numinous power which tries to unfold in man as it does in a sunburst, in a galaxy, in a pine cone or in a flower *is the transforming capacity of creativity*. It can be any responsible response to the challenges of life, as *natural* as the response of the seed to the earth or the response of the bud to the sun. Every one *does* meet with such challenges, every one *can* respond to them responsibly.

Wave Patterns

Let one more, final pattern summarize these decoded messages of patterns.

A pebble dropped into water makes rings of waves, similar to the circle-pattern used to construct the daisy. Two pebbles dropped simultaneously create a more complex pattern (Figure 7). The two sets of circles cross each other like opponents crossing their swords in a duel, but these opponents do not try to cross each other out. On the contrary, they complement each other. Their "duel" is synergetic: new sets of waves emerge from their crossing, their intercourse. These new sets of waves are elliptic, "born" from the centers of the "parent" waves as focal points. The new elliptic waves grow and grow, they become rounder, and rounder, until—beyond the confines of this picture—they too turn into circles.

Simultaneously the parent-waves are transformed. Whereas previously they only grew in *closed* circles, centered around themselves, now they develop also in parabolic arches, each facing its own direction and reaching out—as it were—with open arms towards the infinite. A metaphor of the creative act that changes the creator while changing the world, or a symbol of procreation? Perhaps both.

But in a sense such patterns are more than symbols and metaphors. Symbols and metaphors point to something else beyond themselves, to an idea, to a principle of which they are indirect likenesses, tokens or reminders. However, these patterns are all the "real things." They are patterns of Greater Reality. They are not only reminders and tokens, they are direct imprints of the very same energy which shapes floral tissue, human flesh and bone, dream, poem and wave.

This energy leaves everyone free to change the proportions of his or her unfolding. As one is *free* to choose different pebbles, and throw them in different directions, causing patterns of different proportions to arise in the water, so one is free to choose the proportions in which life shall unfold. For proportions are relationships between parts and wholes, and all human beings are always parts of wholeness that are greater than the sum of their parts. Every moment, every life-situation, every happening is a small wholeness, which is part of a greater one and a still greater one, all related to each other, as the digits of the fingers are related to the hand, the hand to the arm, and the arm to the whole body. It is not only the body which develops from such wholenesses, but also the psyche, which is constantly trying to unfold from the synergy of such opposites as that-which-one-knows and that-which-one-does-not-know: the conscious and the unconscious.

The known and the unknown are like darkness and light. As the wave-pattern is made up of dark and light shades so does Greater Reality unfold from the interpenetration of the conscious and unconscious within the psyche, and in the same way the outer happenings of life emerge from the interactions of one ego with others and with the "ten thousand things of the outer world." This is what one misses in egocentricity: locked into the narrow circle of a limited ego how could one truly interrelate with others? The infinitely varied shades and facets of the *new* can never be born from an unrelated ego; it can never *create*, for *creativity is always a response* born from meeting and interrelatedness.

Inter-relatedness is the hallmark of proportions, while disproportions signal a lack of relatedness. Alienation, the sickness of our times pays no attention to proportions. Proportion is a neglected subject today, a concern only of designers, artists and architects, instead of a matter of general knowledge, as it should and needs be. Indeed, one could say that we live in a *civilization* that has *lost its sense of proportions*. This can be witnessed in the daily life of economics and politics, in pollution, and overpopulation.

Such lost relationships in public life show that dominant Western civilization has riveted too much attention to *one part only* of reality, the one that can be touched, tasted, seen, weighed and counted. This is one part of reality but by no means all. Many have pointed out that the wholeness of reality includes intangibles; feelings, values, intuitions, character, the world of the psyche; i.e. Greater Reality.

Greater Reality is the country of high mountain ranges that surrounds the flatlands and the hill-country where all people live and work. Its snow and ice-covered peaks are not always visible; mostly hidden behind an overcast sky. Those who take reality to be only that which the senses convey or the extensions of the senses—the tools of technology and intellectual concepts—are like the newcomer to a rainy valley, who would not believe that there are snowcovered peaks beyond the hills, where he sees only rainclouds. Then one day the sky clears up and the mountain peaks are there, gleaming with fresh snow in the sunlight, and then he understands why the ancient Indians believed that the Great Spirit lives there!

It is from these mountain ranges that the fresh waters of life-energy come. More channels must be built to bring these waters down into the valleys. Restoring a sense of proportions between the claims of the inner and the outer realms in individual as well as in social life is such channel-building. *Restoring,* because a sense for proper proportional relationships is a native endowment all human beings possess, like the proportional patterning processes and the self-regulating, self-healing powers of body and soul. Without this basic, inborn sense of proportions no one would respond with such delight to nature's patterns in daisies, galaxies and pine cones. There is something in all these patterns that is also within every human being, "naturally," since man *is* part of nature—and this is what triggers the response of delight.

All that exists is part of the tapestry of Greater Reality, which is woven of whole cloth. The happenings are the warps and woofs of this fabric and each life is a thread spun from the light and dark fibers of inner and outer life. Separately these fibers are mere filaments and fragments. What one makes of life, how one responds and relates to others and to the challenges of life which come one's way, this is what makes up the spinning effort that shapes the thread that weaves the fabric, that creates the pattern.

One of the ancient traditions of Qabala speaks about the world of the senses as a fragmented world. It speaks about fragmented human beings, and it says that it is the task of every lifetime to restore as many fragments to wholeness as one finds along the road of life. This is what it means to be a human being.

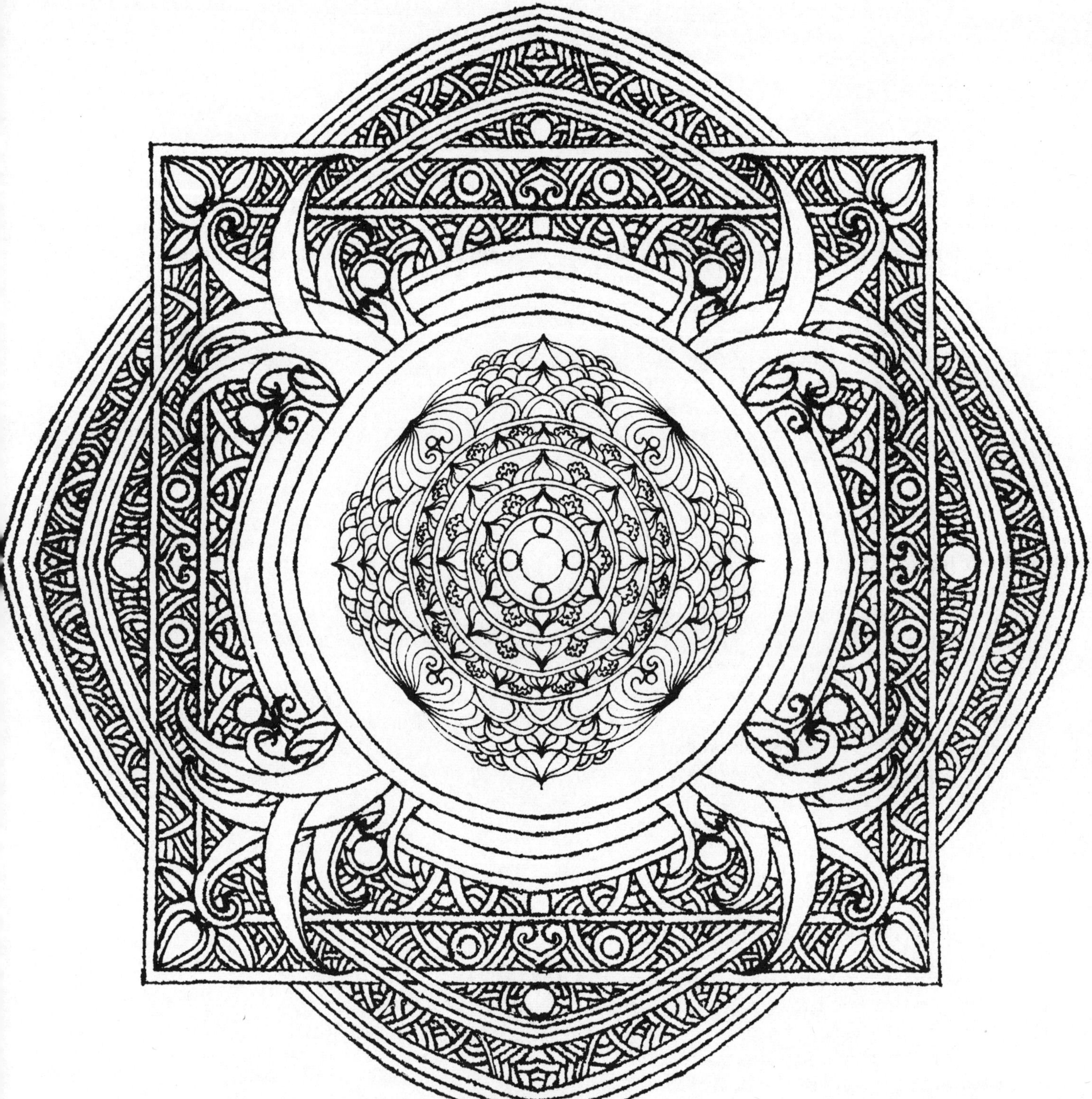

Communion to Community: Relationship as a Path

Robert Hargrove

To become one with anything is to become one with All. When we talk of oneness we mean communion—to come (to) union—oneness together, the Yoga of Relationship. It is a path but it is more than that. It is a condition of being; a consciousness that lies rooted in the heart and yet emerges from the groundswells of daily life.

When any two are united an entity is created in the etheric space that exists between. This entity dissolves all sense of separation between self and others by transforming distance into depth. It is more than just a naked energy. It is deeper than that for it has being. We may call this entity the BEING that is IN RELATIONSHIP. This BEING allows us to transcend the personality level in our relationships because it is not born of the Separated Other.

BEING IN RELATIONSHIP is living for relationship; not for one's own territory—the ego and its strategies. BEING IN RELATIONSHIP is an energy source point for all those who are able to surrender to oneness together. It is the Divine Spark in the human encounter. (Jesus said, "When two or more are gathered in my name, there am I in the midst of them.") The "I" of relationship is a seeing eye dog of the soul. It guides us within and without.

The energy that is to be found in communion is born of oneness. Its power is greater than differentiation; greater than two. As two people turn toward relationship there is a synergistic effect; an inflowing of spiritual power. It is like two horizontal vectors moving toward each other in infinite space. As they come into contact a vertical axis is created that we may metaphorically call spirit. Where there is relationship we can be sure that spirit is entering; that life is becoming full. Where there is separatism we can be sure that the spirit is blocked; that life is hollow and empty.

Emptiness creates fear and fear creates psychological buffer zones between people. Alone and afraid we search for community. It is a desperate search for it is not really community that we seek but a place to hide from ourselves. It is as if we had allowed ourselves to be packed in styrofoam. We want to be let out of our container but more than that we want a place where we can feel safe; where we do not have to worry about being crushed.

Relationship as a path resolves this confusion by encouraging trust—the acceptance of self and others as self. In establishing trust we become keenly aware of the importance of unconditional surrender; friendship and love. Unconditional surrender means that we are committed to relationship regardless of whether our energy is rising or falling, whether we are high or low.

This is particularly important in a marriage. The relationship of a man to a woman always begins with a magical moment in which there is the dramatic ascent of energy. This is one of the highest of flights. It carries with it the sensation of soaring, of righteousness, purity, the expansion of consciousness. (Most of us experience these phenomena at those very special times that we are about to fall in love with someone. Falling in love is an act of relationship—a completely valid approach to spiritual development.)

As the energy goes up it also must fall. And this is where many of our problems begin. Most of us do not know how to deal with descending energy. We interpret it as negativity rather than a grounding. As we begin to fall we experience the sensation of cascading over a cliff of uncontrollable emotion. This literally produces neurotic clinging—the attachment to being high—the inability to relate to a situation that is not basically pleasant.

As we enter into the jaws of relationship we come to realize and accept that life is in fact not always pleasant. But more than that we learn to deal with our own negativity, our highs and lows, all expressions of our own individual bio-energetics.

The body is a wheel of energy. The idea is to fully open up its circuits. (The sensation of being up is the sensation of being opened up. The greater the stimulation that we receive from this, the greater the indication that we have been cut off.) Once we are fully opened up there is no sensation of being high or low, up or down. There is only the free flow of ascending and descending energy. There is only the BEING that is IN RELATIONSHIP.

We begin to share the same feelings toward others that we were once only able to share with our immediate family. It is as if we had entered into a group marriage, as if we had made a long lasting commitment to our own mate. That is what community is all about—to *come* (together) in a *neighborhood*. As communion expresses itself in the ascent of energy, community expresses itself through its descent and grounding. One is representative of a consciousness, the other of a form. When the two are united we have both the vision and manifestation of a Higher Body, a Conscious Society which can bring in the New Age.

Our Living Earth: A Vision of our Relationship with Nature

Rowena Pattee

The pincers of the crane, legs of the wheel,
claws of the bull-dozer
are but extended animal forms.
Our 10-mile long bowel, steel wings and micro-telescopic eyes
reveal a primordial pattern.

A natural growth.
But where is the natural decay and disposal?
Where is the understanding that relates growth and decay
as a complete cycle?
The methods of our living earth are cyclical.
Life without death, growth without decay
is overwhelming, eventually devouring.

How can we know Nature's laws, intuitively, directly,
as men and women unfolding our lives on earth?
First, may we see that everything we do returns to us,
for better or worse?
Second, may we see that everything is equal in its state of *being*?
Third, may we see that there is a hierarchy of forms
in sentient beings, events and consciousness?
Life is a geologist, humanity is a biologist
and the angels must be humanists!
Humanity's gods: first animal, then telluric, then celestial
are reflections of ourselves as our consciousness expands
from the unconscious womb of atomic existence.

Humanity is the consciousness of earth,
arising from the interpenetration of that beyond . . .
symbolized by 'Heaven'
and that below, symbolized by 'Earth'.
We give witness to a movement that embraces all lesser
    movements.
The heavy molten core of the earth gives way
to a thick basaltic mantle
and this in turn to a crust of rocks.

These geospheres are food to the biosphere
that links air and sun with earth.
Life is a film on the earth
resulting from a balanced absorption of solar rays,
water and minerals.
The atmosphere surrounding it protects life
from meteor showers and dangerous radiation from outer space,
while feeding it gases in a balanced ratio
of oxygen and carbon dioxide
from plant and animal breathing processes.
The atmosphere is also the medium in which water,
the necessity of all life,
circulates, thus bathing and nurturing all beings
of this living earth.

The earth's gaseous breath and watery pulse
as well as cave-womb
are the body from which life builds as the skin of the earth.
Her interaction with other planets and stars
is through developed self-consciousness.
Humanity emerges out of the slime of her seas
and caverns of her brain and womb to witness
and communicate with her celestial neighbors.
Earth can be redeemed from her unconscious sleep
by humanity's awakening.

Recognising our terrestrial home,
we become more whole, more human and less self-alienated.
Do we not slay her when we analyze her parts
without equal synthesis and restorative measures?
Technology without restoration is dismemberment
without resuscitation.
The earth is a peopling planet,
but her work of peopling is to little avail
if we people do not recognize her laws, her gifts,
our own inheritance.

It may be that in our sojourn on this planet
all the earth's fuel that we consume and burn,
from polymers to alloys,
from wood and carbon to oil and gases,
will be eaten away.
Where, then may we look but to the sun,
the calyx of the flower of which the planets are but petals?
Yet this light will be blinding
without the complete integration and consciousness
of earth, our bodies, the material substratum
that is the receptor of that light.

The two levels are one: within and without.
What we do to the earth
is what we do to our own bodies.
How we reflect the sun,
is what we do to our own minds.
How we reflect space
is what we do to our own spirits.
To know the earth is also to know the sun and space.
To know our bodies is also to know our minds and spirits.

Is not the sun, equally with the earth,
a pulsing life, radiating and transmitting
from the Center of Centers?
How can it be a dead incandescent body?
As life issues forth from the galaxy to the sun
and to the solar system and our earth,
we also receive life.

Equally, our solar plexus is but a vestigial organ
mirroring our true larger life in the solar system.
Flowers, birds, fish and beasts
are all parts of the sun's life which eat and are eaten.
When we participate in the life of the solar system,
whether by waking, eating, singing, dancing, gardening,
or meditating on the vital center within,
we are already in heavenly company.
Are we aware of it?

The sun knows itself insofar as it knows other stars,
as we know and become ourselves through other humans.
Our realization of the stars in the galaxy
is a function of the galaxies' consciousness.
How can we posit a dead universe
when we ourselves are alive?
There is no bloom on a dead stem.

In each level of life,
the lesser dies to the greater that it may live within it,
thereby being revived by it.
The sun revivifies the planets,
the planets the biosphere which feeds us.
What do we feed?
If humanity is to be consumed,
let it be by angels or gods rather than our own
limbs, teeth, claws and bowels: our technology!
How can we prepare ourselves
to be digestible to angels or gods?
A mere myth or fantasy?

Are we to presume that we are the end product
of the hierarchy of atoms, minerals, plants and animals?
Our perception, limited to our egos and sensorial eyes,
cannot realize the higher levels of consciousness open to us.
This 'seeing' entails death to ourselves as watertight egos.

Our sense may expand, our minds may expand.
We can become as big as we expand, letting go of rigid
    self-images.

Let it happen, by reflecting on the body,
by reflecting on the mind,
by reflecting on the earth and sun,
by asking who?
Who endures through this change,
through this pain and pleasure?
Who? Who?

Nobody.
When the point is reached of no answer,
no ego, no image, no boundary, earth's function begins.
Expanded consciousness, including senses.
The bird wings within. The car races within.
The flower blooms within. The sun glows within.

By emptying, we are filled.
The perception of the wholeness of things,
fills no space and is timeless,
yet emanates in all space and time.
We who emerge from the galaxies, stars and planets,
and the earth's maternal womb and bosom,
are sparks of consciousness
who long for wholeness,
holiness, the true healing.

Expanding to the whole,
We are thrust back to the Numinous Center
being humbled and emptied of projections.
Our lives are totally connected with others.
To serve other sentient beings is serving oneself.
The commonplace world is the setting for divine work.

The modern world is torn, split, fragmented, shattered
materially, nationally, spiritually, culturally.
The industrialized 20th century clings to a pride in progress,
a conceit of sophistication,
and belief in individual achievements.
Such a fragmented self-image brings alienation from the
    sources,
resources and fulfillment of life.
How to work in such a space and time?

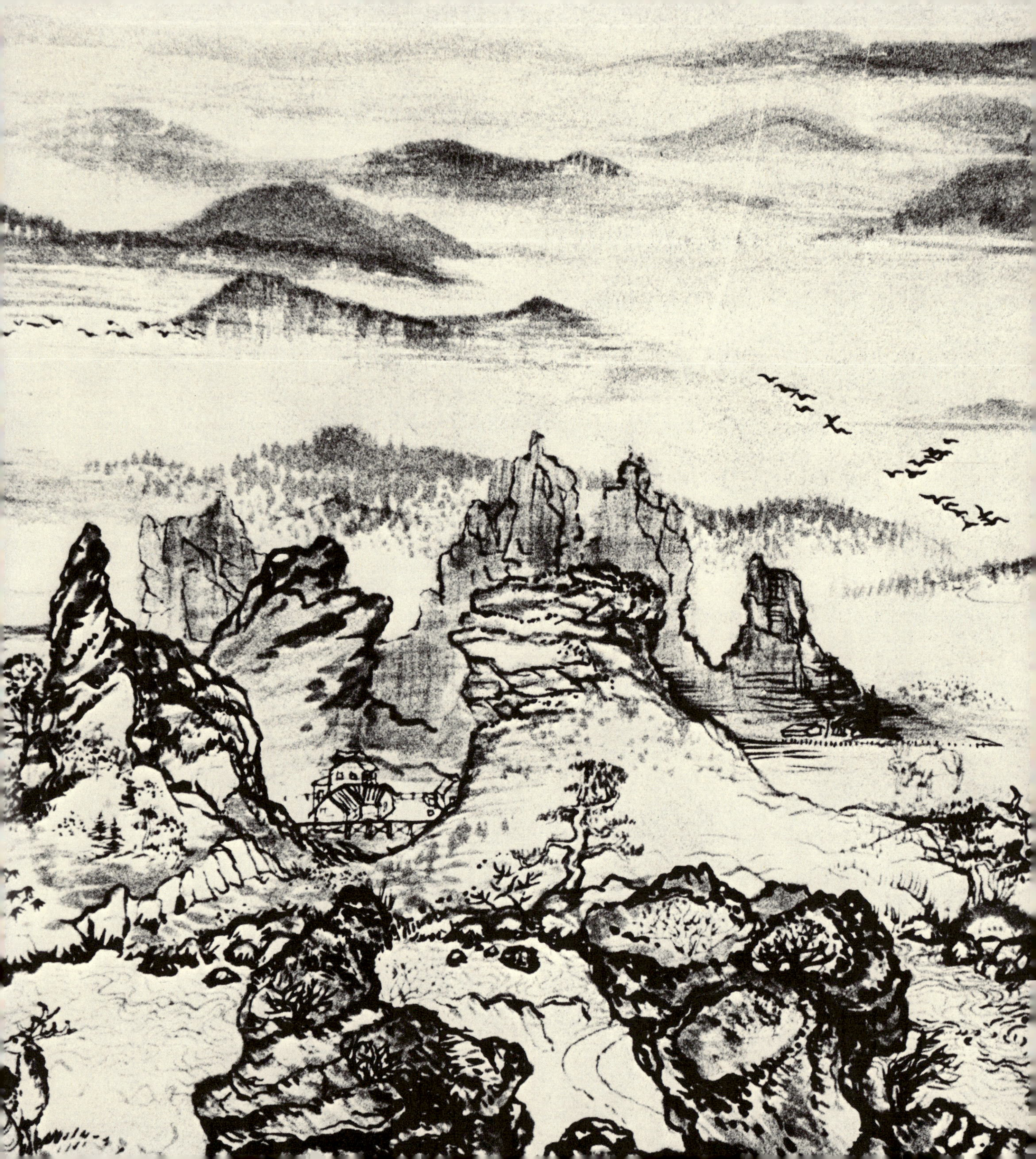

An abundance of opportunity!
We stand in the middle of the humblest of beings on earth
and the vast forces of galactic space.
The energy behind the atom is the same
as the energy behind all galaxies
and that is the same as the energy within our consciousness.
A different pattern. A different wrinkle.

Humanity reflects the 'Above' and 'Below',
'Heaven' and 'Earth'.
We contain both and are contained by both.
We are that intersection of energies
that can direct our own consciousness, our own lives,
but not without penetrating the layers below us,
within our own bodies:
the conditioning, the so-called involuntary systems.
Work on earth, for others,
by understanding ourselves:
the beginning of the way to direct our lives.
The other way, splitting ourselves from earth,
from nature:
alienating, undirective, victimizing and being victimized.

In the lowest we may find the highest.
In the crystal and sea, mountain and flower,
we may live in the refreshing spirit
if we look not with, but through the eye.
Our vastest and most meager bodies
are our capacities through which to realize
the most joyful divine realities.

Contributors

RENÉ DAUMAL wrote and published avant-garde poetry and helped found a French literary review. He trained himself in oriental languages and did translations from Sanskrit, Japanese and English. *Mount Analogue* was his only work of fiction.

GEORGE F. DOCZI was born in Hungary in 1909. He has been an architect and graphic artist in Hungary, Sweden, New York, Iran (where he headed a country-wide reconstruction project) and Seattle. He is one of the Founders and former president of the Friends of Jungian Psychology, Northwest.

HERBERT V. GUENTHER is one of the foremost scholars of Tibetan Buddhism. He has published several books including *The Life and Teaching of Naropa*, *The Jewel Ornament of Liberation* and *The Tantric View of Life*. Since 1964 Dr. Guenther has been Head of the Department of Far Eastern Studies at the University of Saskatchewan in Canada. He resides in Saskatoon with his wife and two daughters.

GEORGE I. GURDJIEFF, virtually unknown in his lifetime, is becoming recognized today as a great pathfinder—a true revolutionary who saw clearly the direction which modern "civilization" is taking, and who set to work in the background to prepare people to discover for themselves, and eventually to diffuse among mankind, the certitude that *Being* is the only indestructible reality.

ROBERT HARGROVE is an ex-truck driver and moving man. After some fascinating years of experience as a booksalesman he went on to become an editor and publisher of *The East West Journal*. He has lived communally with his wife, children and members of the Journal staff for the past two years. He is an occasional speaker and literary agent.

RUTH HOEBEL is an artist and writer living in Berkeley. She is presently collecting material for a literary art journal on madness and the irrational. Her work demonstrates her interest in magic, mythology, the interpretation of dreams. *In pursuit of the infinite.*

GRAHAM PARKES was born in Glasgow, Scotland, in 1949. He studied philosophy and psychology at the University of Oxford, and has been a graduate student in philosophy at the University of California, Berkeley since 1970. He is at present writing a doctoral dissertation on the applications of Heidegger's thought to psychotherapy.

ROWENA PATTEE: "Since a child, I have heard the messages of 'nature'. Now I am conscious that I am an embodiment of that 'nature', reflecting the light that radiates through it. Along the way, many images have been seen, painted, filmed, verbalized and dissolved. Artist, author, teacher, film-maker, mother, all of these are roles that help to facilitate wholeness."

CHARLES PONCÉ is a scholar of symbology. His work includes lectures and writings aimed at bringing these symbols into a living perspective as tools for growth and understanding. Mr. Poncé has authored *The Nature of*

I Ching and *Kabbalah: An Introduction and Illumination for the World Today*. He presently resides in Maine.

DIANE DI PRIMA has read her poetry and taught at leading schools and colleges across the country. She founded the Poets Press in New York City (1964-69). Her writings include: *This Kind of Bird Flies Backwards, The New Handbook of Heaven, Earthsong* and *Loba, Part I*. In 1973 she received a National Endowment of the Arts grant to continue work on her long poem, *Loba*.

GARY SNYDER: "As a poet, I hold the most archaic values on earth. They go back to the late Paleolithic; the fertility of the soil, the magic of animals, the power-vision in solitude, the terrifying initiation and rebirth; the love and ecstasy of the dance, the common work of the tribe... Whatever is or ever was in any other culture can be reconstructed from the unconscious through meditation."

JORDAN STENBERG is a Musician. In the pure Sound with Shape is the Secret of the myriad Manifestations. He expresses through Music, Art and Poetry perception of Truth and Beauty.

VINCENT STUART was born in England and educated at Stowe. He worked with the firm of London Stockbrokers for a short time but quit to study art and book design. He subsequently published hand printed books from his own private press. From 1948-1970 Mr. Stuart was a pioneer London publisher of books on esoteric teachings and allied subjects. In 1968 he helped to establish the Ecology Bookshop in London. He now resides in France, editorially represents Shambhala Publications in Europe and gardens the terraces of his restored home in the countryside.

CHÖGYAM TRUNGPA, RINPOCHE is the former abbot of the Surmang monasteries in Tibet and a meditation master in both the Kagyupa and Nyingmapa lineages. Since 1970 he has resided and carried on his teaching in the United States. He has established several meditation centers throughout the country, an educational center in Boulder, Colorado (Naropa Institute), and a therapeutic community in New York state (Maitri). Trungpa has also written several books, including *Meditation in Action, Mudra* and *Cutting Through Spiritual Materialism*.